Gladys Aylward
THE LITTLE WOMAN

Gladys Aylward
THE LITTLE WOMAN

By
GLADYS AYLWARD
As told to Christine Hunter

MOODY PRESS
CHICAGO

Copyright © 1970 by
THE MOODY BIBLE INSTITUTE
OF CHICAGO

ISBN: 0-8024-2986-6

Moody Paperback Edition, 1974

Printed in the United States of America

Contents

1

China's Millions

MY ONE BIG AMBITION in life was to go on the stage. I had nothing much in the way of education, but I could talk, and I loved to act.

I was brought up in a Christian home and went to church and Sunday school as a child, but as I grew older I became impatient with anything to do with religion.

In those days most girls of the ordinary working class went into "service" because there were few other openings for them. So I became a parlormaid; but in the evenings I went to dramatic classes, as I was determined to save and, by hook or by crook, get on the "boards."

One night, however, for some reason I can never explain, I went to a religious meeting. There, for the first time, I realized that God had a claim on my life, and I accepted Jesus Christ as my Saviour. I joined the Young Life Campaign, and in one of their magazines I read an article about China that made a terrific impression on me. To realize that millions of Chinese had never heard of Jesus Christ was to me a staggering thought, and I felt that surely we ought to do something about it.

First I visited my Christian friends and talked to them about it, but no one seemed very concerned. Then I tried my brother. Surely if I helped him he would gladly go off to China!

"Not me!" he said bluntly. "That's an old maid's job. Why don't you go yourself?"

Old maid's job, indeed! I thought angrily. But the thrust had gone home. Why should I try pushing other people off to China? Why didn't I go myself?

I began to ask how I could prepare to go to a country thousands of miles away, of which I knew practically nothing except that they needed people to tell them of God's love for them. I was told that I must offer myself to a certain missionary society, and eventually I went to this society's college for three months.

By the end of that time the committee decided that my qualifications were too slight, my education too limited to warrant my acceptance. The Chinese language, they decided, would be far too difficult for me to learn.

I left that committee room in silence, all my plans in ruins. Looking back now, I cannot blame them. I know, if no one else does, how stupid I must have seemed then. The fact that I learned not only to speak, but also to read and write the Chinese language like a native in later years, is to me one of God's great miracles.

The committee chairman followed me out.

"What are you going to do, Miss Aylward?" he asked kindly.

"I don't know," I replied, "but I am sure God does not want me to be a parlormaid again. He wants me to do something for Him."

"In the meantime, would you like to help two of our retired missionaries who need a housekeeper?"

"Where are they?"

"In Bristol. Will you go?"

"Very well, but first I would like to say thank you for the kindness of everyone here. I'm sorry I haven't been able to learn much at the college, but I *have* learned to pray, *really* pray as I never did before, and that is something for which I'll always be grateful."

* * *

I went to Bristol to look after a Dr. and Mrs. Fisher. I learned many lessons from them; their implicit faith in God was a revelation to me. Never before had I met anyone who trusted Him so utterly, so implicitly and so obediently. They knew God as their Friend, not as a Being far away, and they lived with Him every day.

They told me stories of their own lives overseas. "God never lets you down. He sends you, guides you and provides for you. Maybe He doesn't answer your prayers as you want them answered, but He *does* answer them. Remember, no is as much an answer as yes."

"How am I to know if He wants me to go to China or to stay in Bristol?" I queried.

"He will show you in His own good time. Keep on watching and praying."

The old missionaries helped me and strengthened me, but still I longed to be "about my Father's business."

Next I went to Neath to work for the Christian Association of Women and Girls. But I did not find enough scope, so I moved to Swansea where I worked as a rescue sister. Each night I went down near the docks and in the dark, unpleasant streets, under the yellow gas lamps, I pleaded with the women and young girls who loitered there.

I went into public houses and rescued girls the sailors had made drunk, and took them back to the hostel. And on Sundays I took as many as I could to Snelling's Gospel Mission.

I enjoyed this work and felt it was something worthwhile, but still the thought of China tormented me. Always it was China! I could not rid myself of the idea that God wanted me there.

I decided that if no missionary society would send me, perhaps I could go out with a family who needed a children's nurse. I went to London to ask advice, but everyone was against such an idea.

"Put the thought of China out of your head," they insisted. "Carry on with the grand rescue work you are doing."

I went back to Swansea depressed and dejected, and in the train I pulled out my Bible. "I don't really know enough about this to start preaching to other people," I said to myself as I turned over the pages. "Maybe I ought to set about really getting to know it."

So I started to read at the very first verse and I read on until I came to Abraham. "Now the LORD had said unto Abram, Get thee out of thy country, and from thy kindred, and from thy father's house, unto a land that I will show thee: and I will . . . make thy name great; and thou shalt be a blessing" (Gen. 12:1-2).

That verse pulled me up sharply. Here was a man who had left everything—his home, his people, his security—and gone to a strange place because God told him to. Maybe God was asking me to do the same.

My next arresting message came when I read the story of Moses. Here again was a man who did something on nothing. What courage he had to set out with a crowd of people who had already shown themselves decidedly difficult! What faith he must have had to obey God and defy all the might of Egypt and the despotism of Pharoah! But Moses had to make the move; he had to leave his quiet home in the desert.

Here I believed I had come upon a really important message. If I wanted to go to China, God would take me there; but I would have to be willing to move and to give up what little comfort and security I had.

Eventually I decided to return to London, get a job as a housemaid, and earn enough money to pay my fare to China.

On the third day on my new job, I was sitting on my bed reading my Bible. I had now reached Nehemiah. I felt very sorry for him and understood why he wept and mourned when he heard about Jerusalem in its great need and could do nothing about it. He was a sort of butler and had to obey his employer just like I did, I thought. Then I turned to the second chapter. "But he did go," I exclaimed aloud, and got up, a strange elation within me. "He went in spite of everything!"

As if someone was in the room, a voice said clearly, "Gladys Aylward, is Nehemiah's God your God?"

"Yes, of course!" I replied.

"Then do what Nehemiah did, and go."

"But I am not Nehemiah."

"No, but assuredly, I am his God."

That settled everything for me. I believed these were my marching orders.

I put my Bible on the bed, beside it my copy of *Daily Light* and, at the side of that, all the money I had—2½d.* What a ridiculous little collection it seemed, but I said simply, "O God, here's the Bible about which I long to tell others, here's my *Daily Light* that every day will give me a new promise, and here is 2½d. If You want me, I am going to China with these."

At that moment, another maid put her head in at the door. "Are you clean crazy, Gladys, gabbling away to yourself like that?"

But I did not care. I felt that God was making me move, and I was ready to obey. The bell rang; my mistress wanted me.

"I always pay the fares of my maids when I engage them. How much did you pay getting here?"

"It was two shillings and nine pence from Edmonton, madam."

"Then take this three shillings, and I hope you'll be happy here, Gladys."

"Thank you, madam."

So, in a few moments, my 2½d had increased by three shillings.

I worked on my days off in other houses as parlormaid, sometimes earning ten shillings or a pound for helping at a

*Two and a half pence, about two and a half cents U.S.

dinner. Sometimes I worked through the night at a society party and earned up to £2.10.* I saved it all.

I went to the shipping offices and inquired about the fare to China. Ninety pounds seemed to be the lowest until a clerk said, "If you want the cheapest, of course, it is the railway overland through Europe, Russia and Siberia."

I went to Muller's in the Haymarket. "How much will it cost for a single ticket to China?" I asked.

The booking clerk's eyes almost popped out.

"China! China, did you say? Now, come on, miss, we haven't time for jokes. What do you want?"

"I want to know how much it will cost for a single ticket on the railway to China."

"Well, I never! All right, I'll find out for you if you will call again in a day or two."

The ticket was to cost £47.10. from London to Tientsin, but I was strongly advised not to try it for there was fighting in Manchuria and there was no guarantee that I would ever get through.

"It's far too much of a risk," the clerk insisted.

"I'm the one who is taking the risk. Will you let me save for that ticket?"

I put three pounds down, and every time I saved a pound I took it to Muller's. At first, saving the fare had seemed almost an impossibility, but in the next few months strange things began to happen.

One day my mistress was going to a garden party with one of her society friends, but at the last moment the friend was ill and could not attend. My mistress sent for me and calmly

*About $7.50.

announced, "Gladys, I want you to accompany me instead of my friend."

"But I can't go to a smart garden party."

"Why not?"

"Have you seen my best clothes?"

"Oh, if that is all, here is the key of my wardrobe. Help yourself to everything you need."

I was feminine enough to enjoy myself thoroughly that afternoon. Dressed from top to toe in clothes far better than anything I had ever worn before, I trotted around with my mistress, feeling quite at home.

When we returned, I was about to take off my borrowed finery, but my mistress said, "You looked very nice this afternoon. I want you to keep everything you have on."

So here I was, provided with clothes such as I could never have afforded myself, and I wore these until I went to China.

Thus in the autumn, because of many, almost miraculous little happenings like this one, instead of taking three years to save the fare, I had already paid the whole £47.10. at Muller's.

Now the question was where in China was I to go? It was about this time that a pastor called at my mother's house and enlisted my help in a campaign at his church. This was the first time I had ever done any real public work.

It was at one of these meetings that an old lady stopped me and said, "I'm interested in China too, because a friend of mine has a friend who has just gone back to that country. Her name is Mrs. Lawson. She is seventy-three and has been a missionary in China for years. She came home after her husband died, but could not settle, so she's gone out again in spite of her age. Now she has written to my friend saying that she is praying earnestly that God will lay it on the heart of some young person to go out to China and carry on the work that she can only begin to do."

"That's meant for me, all right," I said, and immediately I set about seeking the friend who had the letter. I wrote to Mrs. Lawson, and after a long wait the reply came: "I will meet you at Tientsin if you can find your way out."

That settled it for me. The railway was to take me to Tientsin; Mrs. Lawson was to meet me there.

Then hasty packing began. My father insisted that I go home for a few days, and all of them did their best for me. Ivy Benson, a friend who also was a maid, gave me a badly needed suitcase, though it wasn't until long after that I discovered the anonymous gift came from her. My mother sewed secret pockets into my coat and in an old corselet for my tickets, passport, Bible, fountain pen, and two traveler's checks worth one pound each. Another friend gave me an old fur coat and, between them, the family fitted me out with warm clothes.

How good they were to me, I realize more fully now as I look back. How great was the sacrifice my parents were making in allowing their daughter to go off alone to a place thousands of miles away, knowing full well that in all probability they would never see her again. How much I have to thank them for, that they did not try to hold me back.

In my suitcase I had crackers, cookies, tins of corned beef, baked beans, fish, meat cubes, coffee essence, tea, and hardboiled eggs. In an old army blanket I carried my other odds and ends, such as a few clothes, a bedroll, a teakettle, a saucepan, and a small spirit stove which completed my equipment. I had no money to buy food on the way, so I intended to live on what I had with me. The suitcase was heavy, but at least it would grow lighter the farther I went.

2

Moving Out

I SET OFF from Liverpool Street Station at 9:30 A.M. on Saturday, October 15, 1932. As the train drew out and I caught the last glimpse of my loved ones, I felt very small and insignificant. Like Abraham and Moses, I had left all behind me and was moving out into a place unknown with only God to help me.

The journey began well, and I spent a good deal of my time writing a sort of diarylike letter home. We crossed from Harwich to Flushing, then began the train journey through Holland.

When I had stood on Liverpool Street Station with my family, I had especially noticed one couple who were boarding the train, probably because the gentleman had a small goatee. I did not see them again until I entered the carriage at Flushing, when I found myself seated opposite them.

The lady smiled at me. "You are the little girl who had such a crowd seeing you off at Liverpool Street, aren't you, my dear?"

17

"Yes, those were my parents and friends."

"And where are you going?"

"I am going to China."

"To China! Oh, I suppose you have a young man there, and are going to be married."

"No, I have not got a young man. I am going to preach the gospel of Jesus Christ."

Both of them stared at me more closely, but at that moment an attendant appeared at the door. The lady spoke in French and a few moments later the attendant reappeared, carrying a tray containing three cups, a jug of chocolate and a plate of cookies.

"Now you must join us, my dear," the lady said firmly, and I was glad to do so.

"We have just been to the Keswick Convention," she went on. "Now we are returning to The Hague where we have our home. I am English, but my husband is in the Dutch Parliament. We have had a wonderful week of blessing and are going back much refreshed spiritually."

My heart beat with joy. Here were two more people who loved my Lord.

We talked quietly together, and after a time the lady said, "My dear, I am going to make a pact with you. For as long as I live, every night at nine o'clock I am going to pray for you. I want you to write your name in my Bible, and let me write mine in yours. If we never meet again on earth, someday we will meet above."

When they got out at The Hague, the lady kissed me with real affection, and there were tears in her eyes. We had only met for so short a time, yet we had felt strangely drawn to each other.

The gentleman stood at the window and held my hand as he said reverently, "God bless you very richly, my dear, and keep you ever near to Him."

As the train drew away, I looked after them for as long as I could. They seemed to be the last link with the home and people I had known. It was only when I sat down again that I became conscious that I was holding something in my hand. I looked down and found I was holding an English pound note.

Strange to give me that, I thought. He knows I am going where English money is no good. I hid it, however, in one of my special hiding places; and, thousands of miles farther on, that pound note helped me out of a very difficult place. I might almost say it saved my life.

Now, indeed, I felt truly alone. All around me were people wearing different clothes and speaking a medley of languages I could not understand.

When we entered Germany, a railway official tried to ask me questions. I could not understand a word he said. Eventually a German girl came to my rescue. She could speak a little English, and she explained that this man wanted to know if I had anything to declare at customs.

The German girl was very kind and took me to her home to stay the one night I was forced to spend in Berlin. And the next day she showed me around the city before I set off on the long journey via Warsaw, Moscow and Lake Baikal to Harbin.

Of course, there was much that went on around me in the

stations that I could not understand, but Russia depressed me terribly. The people were poor and dirty, and the women seemed to do much of the rough work, even carrying heavy loads.

Always there were crowds of people waiting in the stations, surrounded by bundles which seemed to contain all their household goods. The Russians looked haggard and unhappy. Even the children worked hard, for I saw quite small boys and girls staggering along under heavy loads.

As I sat in the great Moscow station, I saw dozens of soldiers, but how different from ours! They were dirty and untidy, and carried bread under their arms. As they walked about they broke off lumps and chewed them.

I was, by this time, feeling very much alone—a small, strange woman in a very foreign land. But in spite of this, there was a great peace in my heart as I looked back on all God had done for me so far. I truly believed He intended me to get to China to work for Him there.

The days of travel were sometimes monotonous, for I could not speak to anyone, but so far I had suffered no actual discomfort. I was managing very well on my rations, and sometimes at night I was able to rent a bed—a feather mattress from which feathers floated all over the place when I unrolled it.

Our only exercise was to walk along the corridor, except when the train stopped to take on a supply of wood for the engine. Then we all got out and walked about while the train staff sawed up the wood!

As we traveled farther across Russia, water became very scarce. My small teakettleful had to last me all day.

The country became wilder and the train jolted badly at times. I found that I lost my appetite and did not feel so well, but this I put down to lack of proper exercise.

On Saturday, October 22, my seventh day since leaving home, we crossed the border into Siberia. I had to change trains, and now we were in a snow-covered land. I did not think it was possible that there could be so much snow in the world. The sun shone brilliantly, and I sat and marveled at the beauty and wonder of this country with its tall trees, great mountains and wide flat steppes. Yet, I still had to say, "Poor Russia!" It was very, very cold at night, and it was hard to keep even slightly warm.

On Monday, the 24th, a man who could speak a little English entered my compartment. We managed to carry on a rather difficult conversation, but it was good to have someone to talk to. We asked each other many questions and, through him, the conductor was able to tell me that the trains were not running to Harbin, so I would probably be held up at the border. This, of course, gave me a very anxious night. What would I do if I was stranded here, thousands of miles from anyone who could help me? Then I thought, *I am failing my God. He isn't thousands of miles away. He is right beside me. Why should I worry about my journey when God is helping me all the time?* Even if I could have done so, I would not have turned back, for I believed God was going to reveal Himself in a wonderful way.

The train by now was packed with soldiers going to the frontier but, on the whole, I was treated very well. I had known before I set out that Russia and Japan were at war and that the railway service in Manchuria would probably be affected. The soldiers confirmed my fears. They told me I could not reach Harbin, the junction where I had to change to the Manchurian railway, because a train had been captured by the Japanese and the line was blocked.

Later a Russian railway official came to the door of my carriage and spoke to me, but, of course, I could not make head or tail of what he said.

He gesticulated, pointed and shouted, but it was no use; so finally he shrugged his shoulders and departed. The train went on all that day, but during the evening it stopped again. All the soldiers tumbled out; but, having no idea what was happening, I sat still in my corner. After an hour or so, I walked along the corridor and found the train absolutely deserted. The lights were out, even on the station.

Suddenly the sound of gunfire startled me, and I realized that I had come to the fighting line and that the train would go no further. Hurriedly I stuffed my belongings into my suitcase and old blanket and, carrying these, together with my little stove, teakettle and handbag, I climbed onto the platform. I had to move carefully because my teakettle had some water in it, and this was far too precious to spill.

It was bitterly cold. The wind howled around me, bringing with it fine, powdered snow. I sat on my luggage—miserable, cold and hungry—somewhere near the Manchurian border with not a soul in sight. I thought I would freeze to death, and for the first time real doubts came to my mind.

"O God, is it worth it?" I cried.

Like a flash came the answer: "Be not afraid, remember I am the Lord."

So I prayed that God would show me what to do and deliver me—and He did.

I decided that I could sit still in the open no longer, so I stumbled around the deserted station until I found a small hut. Inside I was surprised to find four men—the guard, the engine driver, the fireman and the station porter.

They recognized me because they had tried to make me leave the train at Chita. Once more a pantomime of gesticulation began. They pointed up the line and made popping noises like guns; they pointed to the train and shook their heads to show it would not be moving. At length I gathered that it would wait to take the wounded back, but they had no idea when that would be. Then they pointed down the line and showed me that I would have to walk back. They imitated me carrying my bundles and my teakettle and they laughed; so I laughed too, though actually there was little about my present situation to laugh at.

Eventually they made me a cup of strong coffee which I drank gratefully, and bade me farewell. I tied my bedroll across my shoulders, gathered up my bundles and the precious teakettle and set out to walk along the railroad track back to Chita. I was forced to keep to the track because of the deep snow, but even then it was hard going. On each side towered great forests of pines, their branches creaking under their heavy load of snow.

About midnight I was exhausted, so I pulled myself and my luggage off the track, ate a few stale crackers, boiled water for my coffee essence, then lay down on top of my suitcase, with my old fur coat wrapped around me.

I heard a great deal of barking and howling not far off,

and wondered why anyone had let so many dogs out at that time of night. Never for a moment did it occur to me that the noise was made by packs of hungry wolves. This was one time when my ignorance proved a blessing in disguise.

I did not stay there long for it was too cold. Long before dawn I set off again, and trudged along that entire day, only stopping for short rests, until at last, late in the evening, I saw the flickering lights of Chita far down the line.

With a last desperate effort I dragged myself and my belongings onto the platform and sank down wearily on top of them. People came to look at me and, indeed, I must have looked a sorry sight. I was dirty, untidy and very tired. I sat for hours getting colder and stiffer, but no one seemed to bother.

Just as I was deciding that the best thing I could do was to make some kind of a commotion so that they would arrest me and take me somewhere out of the awful cold, a soldier arrived to make me move on. But I just sat there unmoved. Then three more came and, at last, an official in a red hat appeared. Seeing that I would not move without my luggage, they picked it up and marched me off to a place so filthy that I cannot describe it. The stench was so bad that I almost fainted.

I showed them my passport, and said "British!" So they railed me off from the other people, but all around me were men and women in a horrible condition of filth. I felt ill and almost petrified with fear at the misery I saw everywhere. I thought this was the end of me, and I could eat nothing. Many of my secret pockets had been searched and almost everything of value was taken from me, as well as my luggage; only my little pocket Bible was left. I took it out and held it up to the dusty little light to try to read it, but the light was too dim. However, as I held it up, out dropped a piece of paper—a leaf torn from a daily calendar. And because the print was large and black, I could read, "Be ye not afraid of them—I am your God," a verse from Nehemiah.

How that page got there, I don't know, but after all these years I still have it. To me it was a special message sent to me from God in my direst need. That was my promise; my God would be with me whatever happened. These people could not harm me unless God allowed it.

For some hours I must have been half unconscious until a man grabbed me and marched me out and along a corridor. We passed a Russian soldier who was just having a drink. He pushed the mug into my hand, and I gulped down the cold tea, which revived me and made me realize that I was faint with hunger.

I was taken before an official to be questioned. Another man who was supposed to be able to speak English was brought in, but I had great difficulty in understanding him. Nothing was done for me that day, and I was left under guard, so all I could do was lie down and go to sleep.

All the next day they kept questioning me. My passport had been stamped showing that I had left Chita, so why had I come back again? Of course, I found it almost impossible to explain. Also, it seemed, that they thought I had something to do with machinery. They told me they needed people like me, and tried to persuade me to stay and work in Russia.

This terrified me and I prayed desperately for help. Among my belongings they had found a photograph of my brother in the dress uniform of the army band, and this seemed to have impressed them very much. Evidently they thought I was of some importance.

Eventually I pulled out my Bible and showed them a little picture text I had in it. They seemed to understand, for they gave me a new visa, and another ticket for the next part of my journey.

On Friday I was taken around the town of Chita, evidently with the idea of showing me what a fine place it was. Then I was given my luggage and put into the train with instructions to get out at Nikolshissur Junction, get another train from there to Pogranilchnai, and thence to Harbin. It was the best they could do for me, and I was grateful to them for their efforts to help me.

When I reached Pogranilchnai, there was no train to take me further. The Japanese had closed in, and there was no way through.

As I sat in that station—cold, miserable and frightened— I saw a sight which I have never forgotten. About fifty people—men, women, even young girls—were chained together by hands and feet and were being driven along by guards. Many of them were in tears, the girls almost hysterical. They were being taken to Siberia to work in forced labor camps. From that moment I hated Communism with all my being.

I had to spend all that night on the station. In the morning I saw a train coming the other way going back to Chita, and looking out was a face obviously not Russian. In desperation I cried, "Can you tell me how to get to Harbin?"

Wonder of wonders, he replied in English, "You can't, it's blocked. Go to Vladivostok!"

3

From the Net of the Fowler

THE NEXT TRAIN was so crammed full that I could not get on, but I managed to push my way onto the next one after that, and sank down hoping that eventually I would arrive in Vladivostok.

When, at length, I found myself in the Vladivostok station I had no idea what to do, or where to go. I sat down and prayed. Into my mind came an advertisement I had often seen: "See Russia Through Intourist."

I got up and went to first one and then another saying, "Intourist." Most of them looked as if they thought I was mad, but at last, a man who said he was an interpreter took me to an office, and from there to an hotel.

The interpreter took my passport, saying it would have to be stamped. He seemed pleasant and kind at first, and it was a great joy to be able to have a real wash, to change my clothes and to sleep in a proper bed.

My interpreter offered to show me the town, but the sordid

squalor appalled me. Long lines of people stood waiting for black bread. There was no pavement, and the streets had great holes in them.

The people were very like the Japanese, dark-skinned with tiny eyes. The women were shockingly thin, scantily clad, and usually had heavy babies tied on their backs, as well as great bundles on their shoulders.

After some days I began to feel desperate. I asked the interpreter for my passport, but he tried to put me off.

"Why do you want to leave?" he asked. "You have no money to buy tickets. You cannot get to China. Stay here and help us."

"Why do you want to keep me?" I asked. "Why do you follow me about and watch my bedroom?"

"We need people like you in this country—our new country—new civilization—a land free from the fetters of capitalism."

"No, I will not stay," I replied quickly. "I have seen all I want to, thank you—all the dirt, the squalor, the bad roads, the thin, underfed women, the awful poverty."

"But we will alter all that. That is why we need people like you—men and women who know how to handle machines, who can work in factories and train our people."

"But I am a missionary! I am going to China; I know nothing of machines."

He looked at me so strangely that a cold chill ran over me. "China is far away. You stay in Russia; we will look after you!"

This conversation alarmed me, but what could I do? Without my passport, it was impossible for me to move. Utterly miserable, I felt I must get away by myself for a while. I left the hotel to walk to the seashore. As I went out, a girl came from behind the door and whispered urgently, "I must speak with you at once. I have waited until the Intourist man left you. Walk along, I want to talk."

We walked for a short distance. When no one was near, I said, "Who are you and what do you want?"

"That does not matter," she replied in clear but guttural English. "You want to leave this place? Well, if you don't get out now, you will never get away."

"But what can I do?"

"You must do just what I say. The authorities have no intention of letting you go. Get your things together, and be ready. When an old man knocks at your door, be ready to follow him. Do not ask questions, just follow him."

The girl left and I went back to my room. What was I to do? How did I know that this was not a trap? Whom could I trust?

I was lying on the bed, my head throbbing with anxiety, when there was a knock at the door.

I opened it, and there stood the man who had taken my passport. He held it in his hands but did not offer it to me.

Suddenly I grabbed it from him and threw it behind me into the room, at the same time saying far more boldly than I felt, "You are not coming in here."

"Why not?"

"Because this is my bedroom."

"I am the master; I can do with you what I wish."

"Oh, no, you cannot. You may not believe in God, but He

is here. Touch me and see. Between you and me God has put a barrier. Go!"

He stared at me, then shivered and, without another word, turned and left me.

I sat down on the bed, shaking all over. After such an encounter I had to get away. When I had calmed down a little, I picked up my precious passport and stared aghast at what I saw: "Gladys Aylward, British subject; Profession— machinist." They had altered the word "missionary."

Now I knew that I had to do as the girl said. She had been right about them wanting to keep me. Hurriedly I bundled what was left of my belongings together, and knelt down to pray during the time of waiting.

In the early hours of the morning there was a gentle tap on the door. I opened it a crack and saw an old man standing there. He said nothing but held out his hand for my suitcase, while I took the bundle and the teakettle.

Then we trailed up and down what seemed to me to be miles of streets, stumbling over the uneven cobbles, and at last came to the docks. We sat down in a dirty little shack until it was light, then he left me. I sat alone wondering what was going to happen next. Suddenly I found the girl who had spoken to me the previous day, standing beside me.

"Have you anything of value?" she asked.

"Nothing. Everything of value has been taken from me."

"Have you any money?"

"No."

"Then all you can do is to go into that hut and throw yourself on the mercy of the captain. Plead with him, beg him to take you. You must get on that boat at all costs."

"Why have you helped me like this?"

"You need helping."

"What can I give you? I have no money."

"Have you any clothes?"

"Only what I am wearing. But take these gloves. They are old but they are warm—and these darned stockings. Please take them."

She took them and disappeared.

I went up to the wooden hut and slowly pushed open the door. A Japanese captain was sitting there alone.

"Are you the captain of that boat, sir?" I asked, hardly daring to hope he would understand English. "I must get on it; I must get on it!"

"Speak slowly, please. Good morning. What can I do for you?"

"I want you to take me to Japan, but I have no money."

"You have no money. Have you valuables?"

"No, nothing at all."

"Are you British?"

"Yes, sir. Here is my passport. Please take me with you."

Slowly he examined my passport, then nodded his head. "I see you are in trouble. That will not do. Will you put yourself under my protection and become my prisoner?"

I felt I would far rather be with the Japanese than the Russians, so I willingly agreed.

"You must sign these papers, then you will be safe," he said. "We leave at once."

Just as I was going up the gangway, some Russian soldiers seized me and pulled me back. The sailors stood on the ship, looking down, but they could give me no assistance because they dared not cause trouble.

Desperately I threw my suitcase and bundle onto the deck of the ship and, on an inspiration, pulled out the English pound note the member of the Dutch Parliament had given me at The Hague.

"Look, I buy myself off!" I cried.

The soldiers stared at the note and relaxed their hold. I leaped onto the boat which was just beginning to move, and left part of my coat in the hand of the soldier who had grabbed me. But, at least, I was now under Japanese protection. That Japanese captain was a true gentleman. He was clean and polite, and treated me well.

Some time later, when I had calmed down after my ordeal and had managed to tidy myself up a little, I noticed a woman huddled in a corner, looking desperately ill and miserable.

"Are you feeling ill?" I asked.

She replied in English, "Yes, very ill."

"Is it because you have been seasick?"

"Oh, no, nothing like that! It is because of what has happened. Look at my hands."

Removing a piece of rag, she held out her hands, the fingers of which were torn and bleeding.

"That's where they tore my rings from me."

"Who did that?"

"The Russians. They have stripped us of everything we possessed. My husband is a tea planter. We have been home on furlough and were returning to Shanghai. Every bit of our luggage and money has been taken; we are lucky to be alive."

We talked for a little while, but I did not see this woman, whom I think was a German, again, because I had to stay on a different part of the ship.

Eventually the boat reached Japan and here I found I was the first off because, being a prisoner, I was handed over to the British Consulate. A young man arrived to get me, and told me I was the biggest fool he had ever met! Even to think of setting out on such a journey was crazy! He bought me a good meal, however, and a ticket to Kobe.

I knew I would find help at Kobe, and when I arrived I made my way to the mission hall in a rickshaw. This was my first experience of such a strange mode of transportation.

When I reached the house, I was bowed to, and my shoes removed. This was very embarrassing, for I had a hole in my stocking.

A lady called Miss Santee took me to her home, and how good it was to be in an ordinary, civilized house again! I had a boiling bath in a large wooden tub, then went to bed in a pretty room with a white bed with a blue cover on it, and lighted by a lantern with a red and blue shade.

The next day, Saturday, November 5, I left Kobe after having my ticket exchanged for one to Tientsin. My friends from the mission escorted me to the steamer and explained about me to the captain, so again I was well looked after. I found the food strange and hard to digest. Each person had a little tray with many tiny pots containing soup, meat mixture, salad and vegetables, rice and tea. The other passengers seemed to enjoy mixing all the food together, but I found the rice very hard to swallow.

There were no chairs to sit on and, after removing our

shoes, as is customary, we all sat cross-legged on straw mats on the deck. I found this made me very tired and my back ached.

We passed through beautiful country. High mountains in the distance were covered with snow, while the nearer hills were alight with bright green and glorious red trees. The houses were quaint and decorative, for their gables and gates were hung with flags and banners.

I was beginning to feel very dowdy and grubby, especially among the Japanese women who were so clean and wore beautiful kimonas.

On Tuesday, November 8, the captain sent for me toward evening and told me that over there was China. Away on the horizon, across a muddy, yellow sea, I saw China at last!

Two days later I actually set foot in China, at Tientsin, and immediately made my way to the missionary headquarters. It was bitterly cold, but I was made very welcome, and we all joined together in thanksgiving. I sang, "Praise, my soul, the King of heaven" with a very full heart!

I had expected to meet Mrs. Lawson at Tientsin, but she was many miles away in the mountains. She had sent an escort called Mr. Lu for me, however, so on Saturday we traveled by train to Peking. The trains were very uncomfortable for each compartment held about forty or fifty people, who were jostled about by the lurching train. We stayed overnight in Peking at a Chinese inn, but the dirt and discomfort were appalling.

The next morning we left Yutse by bus as the railroad ended at Yutse, which is the border of Shansi Province. The bus rocked from side to side, and I was amazed that a bus could travel on such roads—up and down mountains, through brooks and rivers—nothing seemed to trouble the drivers. The first night we stopped at Tsinchow, and the following one at Teshchow, where there was a mission station. From here it was two days' journey by mule to Yangchen, where I was told Mrs. Lawson was living.

We crossed three mountain ranges and forded numerous rivers, and I will never forget that first journey with a mule litter. I thought I would be broken in little pieces before we reached Yangcheng, and every bone in my body ached and protested.

When, at last, Mr. Lu stopped the mules before a gateway, and said, "This is Yangcheng," I fell off my animal's back and tottered painfully forward.

Mrs. Lawson came to the gateway, and I bowed, feeling very humble and insignificant. I knew I was dirty, untidy and wilting with fatigue. How would this woman, who had toiled in China for so many years, regard the raw, ignorant recruit who had come to join her?

Actually, I believe she was very pleased to see me, but Jeannie Lawson was Scottish and never showed emotion, so her first greeting was certainly not effusive. As I bowed she said, "And who are you?"

"I am Gladys Aylward who wrote to you from London."

"Oh, yes. Well, are you coming in?"

I had an irresistible desire to laugh, but I managed to turn it into a cough. I had come thousands of miles to join her, and here she was asking me, "Are you coming in?" in just the same tone of voice as my mother's next-door neighbor might have used if I had gone to return a recipe or something I had borrowed.

However, I went inside and took a quick glance at what, I hoped, was to be my future home. It was scarcely attractive. The gateway led into a huge courtyard from which doors into various rooms opened on all sides, but the whole place was littered with fallen masonry, pieces of paper and other rubbish.

"I suppose you will be hungry," Mrs. Lawson remarked and disappeared into the kitchen. A few moments later she returned with a bowl of some queer concoction. I looked at it, I smelled it, and only good manners stopped me from turning away in disgust. Gingerly I tasted it, and thought it was horrible; but it was either that or nothing, and I was very hungry. So, with a great effort, I managed to eat half the bowlful.

We talked for some time, and Mrs. Lawson explained that the house was very old and in a poor part of the town, but that she had come to live here because it was empty and it was cheap. The rent was 2s.4d* a year! No Chinese would live in it because they believed it was haunted by devils. Mrs. Lawson remarked calmly that she had driven them away; at least, she had never seen any since she had lived there! She was trying to get the place cleaned up, but she could not do much at a time.

As she did not suggest taking me to my room, after some time, I asked timidly if I might go to bed as I was very tired after the journey.

*About 30¢.

"Oh, yes, of course, you do just what you wish," Mrs. Lawson replied.

"But where do I sleep?"

"Oh, anywhere!" she said, waving her arm around vaguely. "Anywhere you like."

So I chose one of the rooms, swept the litter on the floor to one side, and put down my bedroll. Then I looked around. There were no curtains, no glass in the windows, and no door in the doorway. I approached Mrs. Lawson again.

"Where do I undress?"

"Why do you want to undress?"

"Because I want to go to bed."

"Oh, I wouldn't bother to undress. It is so much safer to keep all your things on in bed, then they cannot be stolen. As you see, we have no doors to lock."

So I got into bed with my clothes on, and all my things gathered around me, and for the first time went to sleep in the place that was to be my home for many years. In the morning when I awoke I was very glad I had followed Mrs. Lawson's advice, for every window was crowded with curious yellow faces. Evidently word had gone around the town that a foreigner had arrived, and they had come to inspect the strange sight. It would certainly have been very embarrassing if I had had to dress before so many spectators.

4

Among the Mules

YANGCHENG ITSELF WAS BEAUTIFUL—a little Chinese town set in a valley between high, bare mountains. It had a wall all around, many narrow winding streets, and numerous temples which must have been hundreds of years old. It was on the ancient mule track from Hopeh to Honan. There were no real roads in that part of China, only the muddy, uneven mule tracks, and every day long mule trains passed through, or at night stopped in the inns.

There were few trees in Yangcheng, and the mountains were brown and bare, but there was great beauty nevertheless. In winter there was deep snow and it was very cold.

It was nearing the end of November when I arrived at Yangcheng—five and a half weeks after setting out from Liverpool Street Station, but how much I had seen! How much I had learned in those weeks! And above all, for how much I had to worship my God!

Mrs. Lawson had a little money of her own but I had nothing, and we had to exist somehow. Soon after my arrival Mrs. Lawson explained her purpose in living in such a place.

"You see, Gladys, I intend to turn this place into an inn."

"But how, and who will come?" I asked.

"The muleteers will come as they do to other inns in the town. You know what Chinese inns are like?"

I agreed with feeling. I would never forget those in which I had stayed on the way to Yangcheng.

"All the muleteers require is a night's lodging, a place on the *kang*—the long brick bed that is built down one side of the dormitory—an evening meal of millet and flour strips, and some fodder for their beasts. We can hire a Chinese cook for a few pence a week. Then when the men have had food and are resting in the courtyard, we can talk to them. That will be the beginning."

"But how will we get them to come here?"

"You have seen a Chinese landlord standing outside his inn smiling a fat welcome? Then, as the first mule in the mule train passes him, he grabs the animal's head and drags it into the courtyard and, of course, the rest of the beasts follow. Once he has got them inside, he tells the muleteers what a good inn this is, and the muleteers are usually too tired to argue. That will be your job!"

"My job? To grab a mule's head and drag him inside?"

"Yes. You will bring them in, then I will talk to them."

"But do mules bite?"

"Not if you grab the right part."

So we started to get the inn cleaned up and ready for our customers. We got an old man who could cook after a fashion, and then I stood outside, shaking with fright.

The cook had taught me what to say. As I saw the first mule approaching, I yelled loudly, "Muyu beatcha—muyu goodso—how—how—how—lai-lai-lai." That simply meant, "We have no bugs. We have no fleas. Good, good, good. Come, come, come!"

I felt something like a man at the circus shouting, "Come one, come all, come to the fair!"

The first mule I pulled in was fortunately old and docile, but its owner was so frightened that he ran away, though he returned later when he found that his companions had come to no harm.

Soon our inn became known from Hopeh to Honan. Muleteers were the newsmen of North China and they made it known that the inn of the foreign ladies was clean, the food was good, and at night they had long stories told free of charge.

At first Mrs. Lawson or Mr. Lu told the Bible stories while I listened. I was trying very hard to learn the language, but for the time being the most useful job I could do was to look after the mules—to feed them and scrape the filthy mud off them, so that their owners could sit at ease listening to the stories.

Besides the work in the inn, we went out to the villages. On Sundays we got up early and, as soon as the city gates were opened, we went to a strange village. Crowds of people would rush out to stare at us, for they had never seen a white person before. Then we would choose an open space and Mrs. Lawson would start to speak.

Everyone would stop what they were doing and stand outside their homes. Then after a while Mrs. Lawson would let them ask questions.

"Why have you come?" they would ask. "Where do you come from?" "How old are you?" "Is she your daughter?" And so on. Then they would feel our clothes, lift up our skirts to see what we had underneath, and talk excitedly about our feet. Every Chinese woman had bound feet at that time, and our feet always caused much interest.

For several months I struggled with the language. I gave out tracts. I sang to the people, and at night I scraped mud off the mules and helped to look after their rough and none-too-sweet-smelling owners. This was not at all the sort of life I had pictured for myself when I had been in England, but it was a splendid "battle course" for what was to follow.

Mrs. Lawson was, at times, far from well; and I wondered what would happen if she were to die. Never were two people more unlike thrown together in a strange land. Jeannie Lawson was old, dour and dogmatic, while I was young, full of enthusiasm and also had a strong mind of my own. There was only one thing we had in common, and that was the firm belief that God had sent us to this place and had some special work for us to do. How I longed to be able to speak to these people as Mrs. Lawson did, and I set myself to learn several of the Bible stories by heart. By the end of the year, I could understand most of what was said to me, and I could make myself understood. And my repertoire of stories, which I tried out on the muleteers each night, was growing.

At the end of that year Mrs. Lawson became seriously ill, her body simply worn out. There was no doctor within miles, so I had to nurse her to the best of my ability. Near the end she said, "God called you to my side, Gladys, in answer to my prayers. He wants you to carry on my work here. He will provide. He will bless and protect you."

She died soon after that, and I was left alone—the only European in that part of China. But at least God had allowed Mrs. Lawson to live long enough for me to be able to carry on her work.

I kept the inn going, and we held services regularly in the mission hall. I visited houses and gave what medical aid I could to those in need, and I went out into the villages with Mr. Lu to preach in the market places.

But I soon found that the inn did not bring in enough to pay Mr. Lu, the cook, and keep me in food. We only needed a few pounds a year; but now that Mrs. Lawson's small private income had ceased, the standard rate we were allowed to charge for a night's lodging was not enough.

Also, I was very lonely and my position was no easy one. I was only a young woman, and every night my inn was crowded with rough, peasant muleteers. Certainly I could speak their language now; in fact, it was the only kind of Chinese I could speak, for I had learned most of it when listening to them each night. I prayed anxiously, but the way seemed beset with difficulties; I wondered if God was telling me I had to move on from Yangcheng, though where I could go I had no idea.

5

Among the Feet

ONE MORNING the old cook said, "You ought to go and bow to the mandarin."

"But why should I bow to the mandarin?" I demanded.

"The mandarin is a very important person. He can order your head to be cut off."

I certainly did not relish that prospect so I asked, "But how do I bow, and what do I say?"

The cook could not tell me, as he had never bowed to the mandarin himself, but he suggested that he would go out and ask some of the townspeople what to do.

A long time later he came back. "I have asked many people," he said. "They cannot tell you what to do because you are a foreigner, but they all say you must put on your best clothes."

I looked down at the old things I was wearing.

"Then that settles it," I replied thankfully. "I cannot put on my best clothes because these are all I have got."

So there the matter seemed to end, but I felt uneasy because the mandarin was all-powerful in the province. He was a kind of local ruler or magistrate, responsible for law and order in all the villages of the district.

It was just three days after my conversation with the cook that there was a great commotion outside my gateway, and I went out to find the mandarin himself entering my courtyard.

He was dressed in beautiful clothes, with a wonderful headdress on his head. But what alarmed me most was the great, long, curved sword at his side. And behind him were three soldiers also with long, curved swords.

My cook's warning about heads coming off made me approach my visitor very apprehensively. Then began the formal bowing and salutations and expressions of sympathy over the loss of my companion, but finally the mandarin came to the reason for his visit.

"Miss Aylward, I have come for your help."

"My help!" I repeated foolishly.

"Yes, I have come about your feet."

"Not my head?"

"Of course not, it is because you have big feet."

I looked down in astonishment. After all, I only took a size three! "I do not understand, Mandarin."

"I have received a letter from the government—from the new government—and I am much troubled by it. It informs me that by government decree the ancient custom of the binding of women's feet must cease throughout China."

"That is a good thing," I replied. "The poor women are crippled by it."

"The government is holding me personally responsible

for stamping out this ancient custom in this part of the province of Shansi."

"Oh, I see."

"Ah, but you do not see! The government makes the decrees, but how can I enforce them? A man cannot inspect women's feet; a woman must do it. And in all this district there is no woman with unbound feet except you."

"But what can *I* do, Mandarin?"

"Will you become the inspector of feet? It will mean traveling all over this part of Shansi. The government will provide a mule and two soldiers to accompany you. The salary, however, is very low——only one measure of millet a day and a farthing to buy vegetables."

I could hardly believe my ears. Was this God's plan for me? Was this how He was providing for my simple needs?

"I will do as you wish, Mandarin, but you understand that I have come to China to tell your people about the God I worship. If I inspect the women's feet, I shall use the opportunity to preach in all the lonely villages."

"I understand and I acquiesce. A man's gods are his own affair; I have no religious bias. Also, from the standpoint of this government decree, your teaching is good, because if a woman becomes a Christian she no longer binds her feet."

"Then I gladly accept your offer."

The mandarin made his farewell, and with much bowing he departed. I went into my room and fell on my knees in humble worship and thanksgiving. The way was clear. My place was here; God's plan for my life was unfolding before me.

Yangcheng remained my center and, between them, Mr.

Lu and the cook carried on the work of the inn, for sometimes I was away for a week or more at a time. My two soldiers and I would set out in the morning with our mule,
which was carrying a good supply of dried food, and travel
all over that mountainous province.

When we came to a village, the soldiers went on ahead and
summoned everyone to the village clearing. Then they repeated the mandarin's instructions, announcing that foot-
binding was now illegal and a punishable offense.

The men would shuffle and look uncomfortable. They
liked their women to have little feet; it was a sign of beauty
and had always been done. Then the soldiers would shout,
"If any child's feet are bound, her father will be taken to
prison. Ai-weh-deh is the government foot inspector; she
must see the feet of every woman and child. Any woman who
refuses to have her feet examined will be punished."

Ai-weh-deh was the Chinese name I had been given. It
meant "virtuous woman."

Then I would start to talk to the people. I would tell
them a story—very often a fairy story like Little Red Riding
Hood. I would get them all laughing and happy and teach
them to sing a chorus after I had explained the meaning of
the words.

Then I would talk to them about their feet.

"You know that boys' feet and girls' feet are all alike; if
God had wanted girls to have little, stunted feet He would
have made them like that. But instead He made them all the
same. And now the government says the feet of girl babies
must be allowed to grow naturally. They must not be bound.
Any women who bind their babies' feet will be punished.

If you men let your daughters' feet be bound, the soldiers will take you away."

It was too late to do anything to help the older women, but something could be done for girls in their teens. I made them unbind their feet, and ordered them to wear shoes that were big enough for them. They hated the idea at first and thought that it would ruin their chances of getting a husband. But the soldiers told them, "You can either unbind or go to prison. Please yourself, little sister, it is very comfortable in prison."

Sometimes in the evenings the villagers would come to the inn where I was lodging for the night and ask me to tell them more stories and teach them more choruses. So for months and then years I traveled around to village after village until I became known and welcomed and made many friends. I was called "The Storyteller" and the villagers never tired of hearing the Old Testament stories told over and over again.

As I look back, I am amazed at the way God opened up the opportunities for service. I had longed to go to China, but never in my wildest dreams had I imagined that God would overrule in such a way that I would be given entrance into every village home; have authority to banish a cruel, horrible custom; have government protection; and be paid to preach the gospel of Jesus Christ as I inspected feet!

Gradually there were ones and twos converted here and there and in each village a little group gathered—the beginning of a small church. So through the next years as the gospel was preached, the practice of foot-binding ceased, opium-taking was reduced, and a witness to the saving grace of Jesus Christ was set up in many places.

I now lived exactly like a Chinese woman. I wore Chinese clothes, ate their food, spoke their dialect, and even found myself beginning to think as they did. This was my country now; these northern Chinese were my people. I decided that I would apply to become a naturalized Chinese subject. In 1936 my application was granted and my official name was Ai-weh-deh.

6

Ninepence

THOUGH I HAD MADE FRIENDS among the Chinese, I still
longed for fellowship with someone of my own kind. I had
prayed for years that someone would come out from England
to share my work, but no one came, so I went on alone. The
dreams I had had long ago of a husband and children of
my own were fading. It looked as if the Lord intended me
to walk alone all my days, but sometimes the isolation of my
position weighed heavily upon me.

One day I was feeling utterly depressed, and had prayed
almost in desperation that God would send someone to help
me. I had been out to the villages and was on my way to
make my report to the mandarin who, through the years, had
become a firm friend. I noticed a woman with a child sitting
by the roadside. The sun beat down mercilessly upon the
child's bare head, and she looked desperately ill. She was
thin, horribly dirty, and covered with sores.

"That child shouldn't lie out in the sun like that," I said, looking down at the miserable little body.

"She is my child. It is no business of yours what I do with her."

"Woman," I said sternly, "it *is* my business. I am Ai-weh-deh. If you do not attend to that child she will die."

"Well, if she does, I can get another to take her place to-morrow, or maybe the day after."

I stared from the woman to the child in horror. Stories I had heard of children being bought and sold must have been true ! A woman such as this revolting creature could buy a child and then let it die without any sort of punishment.

As I stood gazing at the child, my eyes filled with tears. The woman leered at me and said in a whining voice, "You can have her if you like for half a crown."*

"No," I said, though I could scarcely speak.

"Two shillings,† then," she wheedled.

"I haven't got two shillings," I replied angrily. "And you should be ashamed of yourself. You know very well that another couple of hours in this sun and that child will be dead."

I turned and went on my way to the mandarin's house. I was too angry and upset to give him my report, but instead I poured out a tirade against conditions that allowed traffic in helpless infants.

"You and I can do nothing," the mandarin said calmly. "Such things must be stamped out by new government laws just as foot-binding has been dealt with."

*About 35¢.
†About 28¢.

When I returned home, the woman still sat there.

"A shilling,* lady," she said as I came near. "You can have her for only a shilling."

Again I looked at the thin, miserable, unwanted scrap of humanity and my heart ached for her sufferings. I put my hand into my pocket and found that all I possessed was five Chinese coins, about the equivalent of ninepence in English money. I held them out.

"This is all the money I have."

The woman grabbed the coins, picked up the child and pushed her in my arms.

"She is yours, lady. I knew you had a kind heart."

So Ninepence came into my life and helped to fill the aching void. Here was someone I could love and care for—someone whose eyes lit up when I approached. I washed her and fed her, and within a few days she was a different child and was making the place seem like a home. A few months later Ninepence brought in a little boy from the streets; he, in turn, brought in two more, and so on. Before long I had about twenty children dependent on me, and often there was very little to feed them on. But we never actually went without and, at least, I could not complain of being lonely. Indeed, often I craved for a few moments of peace.

*About 14¢.

7

Mrs. Ching

ONE DAY AS I TRAVELED, the road was especially rough and stony, for it led straight across the mountains. The mules were laden with provisions and bedding, and I was sitting right on top of the pack on the leader of the mule train.

I was hot, tired and dirty and would have liked a bath and a comfortable bed, for we had traveled a long way since leaving home. But just ahead lay a village with a bad reputation, so I had more important things than baths to worry about.

The two soldiers who had been appointed to act as my bodyguards walked solidly along beside the mules. They scarcely spoke, but I believe they were secretly proud to be in charge of this strange foreign woman. They had found that although I was small they had to do as I told them. They had also found that I always told them the truth, and that I treated them kindly. In time, my soldiers and I became quite fond of each other.

As we entered Yuan Tsun (Luster Village), no one was in

sight, until a muleteer shouted, and out ran the innkeeper. We were taken into a filthy, dark room, smelling horribly of animals. The innkeeper looked at me askance when told that I was Ai-weh-deh, and why I had come.

"I will see the women tonight," I said.

"Wait until tomorrow," the innkeeper suggested.

"If I do, word will get around the village, and the women will have time to hide the little girls. We will begin at once," I replied firmly.

So my two soldiers and I started out, the innkeeper muttering curses after us.

I told my soldiers to hurry, for I felt sure that the innkeeper was already sending messengers around the village. We saw several women and inspected the children, and ordered that there must be no more bound feet. Then we came to a house where there was no glimmer of light. I felt that here there was going to be a struggle.

I knocked and called. There was absolute silence. Then one of my soldiers banged on the door, shouting, "Open up, this is Ai-weh-deh who has been sent by the mandarin."

Still silence.

"Call and tell them that I am coming in through the window if the door is not opened," I ordered.

The door opened a crack, and a tiny, frightened face peered round it.

Immediately I pushed the door wide, and stepped inside.

"Now, woman," I said boldly, "I know what you are hiding, because the God I worship has told me all about it. So bring those little girls out at once, or I will search and find them myself."

The woman scuttled away and returned with a poor, thin, terrified little creature about four years old. She could not stand for her little feet were in the process of being bound and her eyes were full of tears. She crouched pitifully on the floor.

I picked up the child, the tears now streaming down my face at the sight of her misery.

"Is all well?" shouted the soldiers at the door.

"All is well," I replied and sat on the *kang* (brick bed), with the child on my knee and quickly unbound her tiny, hot, aching feet.

"Fetch some warm water in a bowl," I ordered.

"Oh, that is good," the child murmured, her tears turned to smiles as I massaged and bathed her feet. I started singing quietly and the child relaxed sleepily in my arms. Suddenly she started up.

"What about Precious Pearl, and Jade Lily, and Glorious Ruby and Crystal?"

"They will come too," I said gently and put her down.

"Bring the other children," I ordered the woman, who had stood staring at me all this time.

"There are no other children," she declared. "That child talks stupidly."

Going to the door, I called to my soldiers, "There are other little girls, but this woman will not bring them out."

"There are no more children," she shouted.

"Then we will search," the soldiers said firmly.

"Very well, I will bring them," the woman said sulkily, and brought out four others.

I unbound all their tiny feet, and bathed each one, singing to them and loving them.

At first they were cowed and terrified, but gradually their fear disappeared, and before long all five little girls were peacefully asleep.

Feeling that I dared not leave these children, for I did not trust the woman who had charge of them, I told the soldiers to fetch our belongings from the inn. They made themselves as comfortable as possible in the outer room while I shared the *kang* with the five children and the frightened, grumpy woman.

A little lamp containing peanut oil was left burning, so the room was not in complete darkness. In the middle of the night I awakened to see the woman sitting up, weeping bitterly. Creeping over to her, I asked her what was the matter.

"I am frightened of my master," she sobbed. "He will kill me when he returns."

"I will deal with him," I said boldly. "I have been sent by the government, and my two soldiers will see that he does you no harm."

"You cannot understand," she moaned. "He is wicked and cruel. He bought me, and now he has bought these children. As soon as their feet are ready, he will sell them to whoever will pay the most money for them."

"I know Someone who will take all your fear away," I replied. "Jesus Christ has sent me to help you. I will tell you about Him, and He will comfort you."

Lying beside this poor, frightened, lonely woman, who had been bought like a mule and was now kept like a slave, I told her the story of God's great love for poor creatures like herself, of Jesus who loved her and died for her; and I told her how happy she could be.

This wonderful news seemed too good to be true. Never had she heard anything like this before. How much she longed for this Jesus to help her and to save her from the terrible beating her master would give her when he heard that she had let Ai-weh-deh into the house.

For two more days I went from house to house with my soldiers, returning each night to the home of the five little girls, where Mrs. Ching was living in dread of the moment when her master would return.

On the third morning, I roused them all as soon as it was light.

"I am going to take you all to live with me in the city in my mule inn where I have other little boys and girls," I told Tiger Lily, Precious Pearl, Jade Lily, Glorious Ruby and Crystal. "You will learn to read and to sing and to love Tien Fu (your heavenly Father), who sent me to look for you."

"What about Mrs. Ching?" they asked. They did not love this woman, for she had been cruel and unkind to them, but they knew what would happen if she were left behind.

"Mrs. Ching will go with us too," I replied.

The children rushed around excitedly on their unbound feet, full of happy expectation. Already they looked very different from the cowed, grubby, little waifs I had first seen.

My two soldiers seemed quite glad to take such a large crowd under their protection and all of us, with the exception of Mrs. Ching, set off gladly for home. She, poor woman, believed she was being taken to prison. To her the city was an awful place. There would be no one to speak for her.

Her master would follow her because he had paid money for her, and he would either leave her in prison or drag her back to the village and beat her continually.

On reaching the city, it seemed as if hundreds of children rushed out to greet us. Actually there were only twenty-four, but they jumped and shouted and knocked each other over in their efforts to be the first to reach me.

The old man who acted as cook looked calmly on. He was just as glad to see us as the children, but he was too old to shout and run.

Bao Bao (Precious Bundle), the youngest, somehow reached me first, and I took him up in my arms. I was as delighted to see my dear children as they were to see me.

Gradually they quieted down, and politely, one by one, I introduced the newcomers. Then I handed the five awed little girls over to a "big sister," who took them away to be washed and fed and put to bed.

Mrs. Ching watched all this in silence. Now she came nearer and said, "When are you going to send me to prison?"

"Prison!" I exclaimed. "I am not going to send you to prison. This is going to be your home. You will have to sleep with me, I am afraid, as the inn will be full tonight."

Mrs. Ching stared in amazement. "You mean you want me to live here with you? You know how mean and cruel I was to those little girls. I refused your God, I was rude to you, yet you still want me?"

"Yes, I want you because my God wants you," I replied.

Mrs. Ching turned away and stumbled into the kitchen, where Chang, the old man, was stirring a huge pot. I followed and stood near the door, wondering how Chang would treat this newcomer.

"You can stir this," he said without looking up. "I want to make a little pot of nice thick porridge for my dear one."

"Your 'dear one'! An old man like you has a 'dear one'?" Mrs. Ching exclaimed.

"Yes, I am sixty-eight, and I love for the first time in my life, and not even one of my own race. But I am not ashamed. I love her because she told me about Jesus."

"Oh, you mean Ai-weh-deh?"

"Who else? I was a lonely, bad-tempered old man until she came to my village. I listened to her stories and her songs, and I was interested. I learned that she needed a cook, and here I am. I cannot cook, but that does not matter. I do my best. I love these children, to whom Ai-weh-deh is now more than father and mother. Oh, yes, sometimes they are naughty, but Ai-weh-deh says God loves naughty, wicked people so we must do the same."

At that moment the children swarmed in from the other doorway, holding up their little bowls to be filled. Then standing around we sang:

> Come and eat, for Jesus invites you;
> He loves and feeds you. Just trust Him.
> Amen

Just as they were finishing eating, there was a commotion outside the inn, and in came a crowd of muleteers with their dirty, tired mules. Mrs. Ching stared in bewilderment as these rough men settled down with their bowls of food.

It was almost dark when I went out into the crowded

courtyard and began to talk to the children and men who were gathered there. We sang a chorus, I said a short prayer, then I told the old, old story of God's great love for man. They sat there in the twilight, listening intently, only the stamp of the mules disturbing the peace of the evening.

Then the children hurried off to bed and, one by one, the men fell asleep. Gradually the inn settled for the night. Only Mrs. Ching and I, in our little room, were awake. Suddenly she burst into tears.

"I have been a wicked woman, Ai-weh-deh," she sobbed, "but I want to be different. Teach me how to live for the Jesus you talk and sing about. Ask Him to forgive my sins and give me peace."

Together we knelt down and prayed to the loving Saviour who had seen this poor woman's misery, and soon she was radiant with joy.

After a great struggle, we were able to buy Mrs. Ching from her horrible master. Soon she was telling other women like herself how Jesus Christ had saved her and changed her life from one of misery to one of joy.

"My heart was bound up tight with sin, like I bound up the feet of the little girls," she said. "Now I am free and my heart can grow big with happiness."

8

The Lull Before the Storm

THE MANDARIN PROVED HIMSELF a true friend, and often we had long and serious talks together. He was an educated man, and thought deeply. He asked me many questions, some of which I could not answer.

One day he said, "You send your missionaries into our land, yet our country is far older in civilization than yours. You look upon us as a nation of barbarians, do you not, Ai-weh-deh?"

"Not barbarians, but those who need the true God."

"We have produced great art and philosophy. The Mandarin speech of China is more beautiful and descriptive than any other in the world. Our poets were singing and writing in Chinese when Britain was an uncivilized island on the edge of the then known world, yet you come to teach us a new faith. You try to convert us to a new religion."

"Mandarin," I said, while in my heart I prayed for this man whom I believed to be really searching for God's salvation, "look out of this window. Look at that coolie staggering under a load far too heavy for him. Look at the peasant over there in the field, his wife in the mud hut, the naked, hungry children. Think of the poverty, the misery and the starvation all around us."

"But it has always been in China; it always will be so. It is the will of the gods."

"Not the will of *my* God. He will bring hope and happiness."

"Ai-weh-deh, you preach and you work for your God, but I do not think you will make a ripple on China's consciousness as great as the ripple a gnat makes when he touches the surface of a great ocean."

"Jesus Christ, the Son of God, was born two thousand years ago. He was a Baby born of a humble mother in a stable in an insignificant village. Yet, because of the ripple He created, I am here, many thousands of miles away from my own land."

"You have learned the intricacies of our beautiful language exceedingly well, Ai-weh-deh."

"I think perhaps I understand it better than my own language, Mandarin. I belong here; I feel I am needed here."

"Yes, you are needed. I do not understand all you teach, Ai-weh-deh, but I admire what you have done for us."

"But I want to do more, Mandarin. You have given me permission to visit the prison, but the conditions are terrible. My country is not as old as yours, but our people would not tolerate such conditions as exist here, even for their criminals—the poor, manacled, filthy, half-starved wretches!"

"But they *are* criminals, Ai-weh-deh."

"Yes, but that does not mean they should be treated like pigs, neither does it exclude them from God's mercy and forgiveness. Poor, unhappy China!"

"You pity us, Ai-weh-deh?"

"I pity you because the love of God is not shed abroad in your hearts. Jesus said that for His sake we should visit those in prison, clothe the naked, feed the hungry and care for the fatherless. 'Inasmuch as ye have done it unto one of the least of these my brethren, ye have done it unto me.' "*

"Then that is why you took home that child from the roadside?"

"Poor little mite! If I had not taken her, she would have died."

"Children die like that every day—hundreds of children. But now you are her mother."

"Yes, I am her mother."

"You are a great figure in my province, Ai-weh-deh. You care for the sick; you help at childbirth; you visit our criminals; you mother our unwanted children. In every lonely village, in every part of the mountains, you are welcome; yet you came to us a stranger and a foreigner. This must be a strong faith of yours, Ai-weh-deh."

"It has borne the weight and misery of two thousand years, Mandarin. No amount of persecution has been able to kill it."

* * *

During the Chinese-Japanese War the arrangements for medical care of the wounded were of the most primitive kind. There were no Red Cross and no field hospitals, although in this part of northern China there were vast numbers of

*Matt. 25:40.

wounded Chinese constantly needing attention. For this reason a body of Christian pastors, evangelists and teachers, who would not take part in the hostilities themselves, banded together in a unit to help the wounded in transit. It was a fine body of men who willingly risked dangers and discomfort that they might bring help, both physically and spiritually, to those in distress.

Because at that time I was living almost on the battlefront and often had between thirty and forty wounded men lying in my courtyard, I applied to this unit for help. My own medical knowledge was slight, my supplies negligible, and practically the only helpers I had were my adopted children. The patients had to be fed and attended to, and I felt that someone far more capable than myself should take over this work. We were at the middle period of the war when I made this application, but for some time I got no reply.

We were also busy arranging for our annual convention. Maybe it seems strange that when the country was in such a state of upheaval and traveling was so dangerous that we would invite people from all the surrounding districts to leave their homes and travel over mountain roads to attend a week of services. But we prayed for great blessing, and continued our preparations.

As our guest speaker we had invited Chang Meng En, a very fine evangelist and the pastor of a church three days' journey away. At that time we were in Free China and his church was in occupied territory, but we hoped and prayed that he would be able to attend. At last the first day of the convention arrived, but not the guest speaker. Months later we learned that the Japanese had refused him permission to travel.

The Christians came pouring in, some having walked for over a week, some for five days. They were thirsting for fellowship and prepared for great blessing.

After the welcome meeting on the first night, the guests were shown to their rooms and given food. Those of us who were the leaders were on our knees in the chapel seeking God's guidance in this awkward situation. By tomorrow there would be over a thousand people in the compound. What were we to do without a guest speaker?

Suddenly a child pulled my garment. "Ma, there is an important man seeking you."

I hurried out to find a tired, dusty man in a soldier's uniform awaiting me. He saluted politely.

"Madame, I have been sent to discuss your appeal for help for the wounded in this district."

"Oh, dear!" I said impatiently. "I cannot discuss this with you at this moment. Tonight we have started a week's convention, and I shall have no time until next week. If you will sit down and rest, my little boy will bring you food and show you somewhere to sleep. I must return to the chapel." Back I hurried, and again fell on my knees.

A few moments later a new voice began praying in a different dialect, but with what power he prayed! We opened our eyes, and I was amazed to see that it was the dusty soldier who was praying among us. As we rose, I grasped his hand. "You are a Christian!" I said joyfully.

"Of course! I would not be in the group to aid the wounded soldiers if I were not."

The only place for him to sleep was at the door of my room, which was already packed full of women and children. And when we got up in the morning, he was gone. After the prayer meeting, which lasted two hours, there was breakfast. This was followed by a half hour of singing; then came the first real meeting of the day. The place was packed to suffocation. The people waited in eager anticipation while we leaders were still uncertain as to what line to take. Then in came our soldier in the same worn, gray uniform, but looking clean and fresh because he had bathed in the river.

He stepped on the platform and began to speak. Never will I forget the hush and the sense of great power that came upon us. When, at the end, he asked for Christians to rededicate their lives, everyone fell on their knees, and prayers came from all over the building.

For five days the gray-clad figure of Jonathan Wen led us. We had no time to bother about eating or sleeping. We had prayed for revival, now it had come like a mighty flood. Every day dozens accepted the Saviour for the first time. Men and women from the city wandered in to see what it was all about and before long they, too, were on their knees weeping for their sins and praying for God's forgiveness. How great was our joy that, at last, the years of faithful sowing were resulting in this abundant harvest.

On the final evening Jonathan and the leaders led a farewell meeting. We knew we would never meet again because word had come that the enemy was pushing closer and would be on us very soon.

The women, one by one, said good-bye to me, and everyone went quietly away. I was so exhausted that I fell fully clothed on the bed beside the children.

Very early I was awakened by a strange noise. Thinking it was enemy bombardment, I picked up Bao Bao, the youngest child, and rousing the other children, we rushed out to the front courtyard which was very large for it had once been three camel inns. Instead of an enemy plane, a wonderful, amazing sight met my eyes. Hundreds of men and women were praying—some kneeling, some standing. A power that I can only liken to that of Pentecost swept over that place. In a moment I, too, was on my knees, awed and full of great reverence. Beside me was a woman who, with tears running down her face, was pleading with God for her husband. Suddenly the dawn began to break and over the compound was a great "Hallelujah Sam Mei Chu" (Praise the Lord).

As the morning lengthened, we said farewell once more, and this time they left in twos and threes on their long trek homeward.

Two days later the Japanese arrived, but all our guests were by then well away into the mountains, taking a little of heaven's glory with them.

One day, weeks afterward, as I was singing some choruses, a Japanese officer approached and said, "People in the mountain villages sing your songs. I have heard them."

I nodded and smiled, but said nothing. The enemy might be moving across our country into the mountains, but before them had gone God's Holy Spirit. He had sent to us a messenger of His own special choosing, and had strengthened our feeble faith before the time of greater testing.

9

At War

ONE MORNING we were arrested by an unusual noise. The people ran out to see many little silver planes in the sky, shining in the sunshine. They shouted and waved excitedly, for none of them had ever seen an airplane before.

Then the planes flew low over the town, backward and forward, dropping their bombs. We were holding our morning service when one hit the mission house, and I could recall nothing more until I was dragged out of the ruins some time later.

When I had pulled myself together, I dug in the debris until I found my little first-aid box. But all it contained were a few small bandages and a bottle of iodine; and hundreds were dying, if not already dead, all over the town. It was heartbreaking, and a terrible introduction to the awful ravages of war which we were to endure again and again.

The Chinese were dazed and unable to organize any effectual sort of service. There was the never ending work of

67

burying the dead, comforting the living, attending to the wounded, looking after the babies—who so often were born, only to die after a few hours or days—and helping the poor, stricken mothers.

The inn was so badly smashed up that we had to move in with another missionary who had come into the area a few months before. From there, for the time being, I continued my work of evangelizing the villages. Sometimes, Mr. Lu, the Chinese evangelist, accompanied me, but more often I took two or three of my children with me.

My travels took me far afield and sometimes I entered villages occupied by the Japanese. They did not interfere with me, and some of the Japanese soldiers came to my meetings. They did not understand Chinese, but they joined in the choruses. One or two of them were Christians already, so they sang in their own language.

Yangcheng was actually on the battlefield itself, and was forever changing hands. When the Chinese army moved up and camped near, I visited the soldiers in their quarters and was invited to have tea with the general and his wife. They were most friendly, and soon I was one of their frequent visitors.

On one occasion the general was poring over his maps when I was in the room.

"I wonder if they have reached this place yet," he said, pointing on the map.

"Oh, yes, I was there a week ago, and they were all over the place," I replied. "They came to my meeting."

After that I often gave information of enemy movements. I suppose I was a spy, but I was Chinese and the Japanese were our enemies. They had despoiled our country, disturbed our way of life and killed our friends.

Often when I was out visiting my village congregations I found out where the Japanese were and what regiments were being used, and I passed the information on to the general. I was able to go out quite openly to do my work as an evangelist, often in enemy-held territory, and nobody interfered with me.

From 1938 onward we were in the middle of the fighting. Four times Yangcheng changed hands. First the Nationalist armies would take it, then the Japanese, and each time we had to flee to the hills and live where we could, in caves or holes in the ground, and eat if we were lucky.

Each army, in turn, looted the city, until none of us had anything left. Yet, when the army left the city, we went back to the ruins of our homes, only too thankful to get there. I had two planks for a bed, two stools, two cups and a basin. On the broken wall still hung a small card which said: "God hath chosen the weak things—I can do all things through Christ who strengtheneth me." And it was true! I had passed through the fire, but He had strengthened me.

For a long time I had been unable to get any news through from England because what postal service there had been was now broken down completely. It was 1941 before I heard that there was war in Europe. It was strange to think that my own people were enduring the same sort of torture as I was, here among my Chinese people.

One day my old friend the mandarin sought me out in the caves where I was caring for a crowd of refugees.

"It is good to see you are still alive and well, Ai-weh-deh," he greeted me with real feeling. "I have come to bid you fare-well. I am leaving this province, and another governor will take my place."

"Oh, I am sorry."

"I have watched you ever since you came, Ai-weh-deh. You love all our people, and you work hard for them."

"It is God's will that I do so, Mandarin."

"That I have come to know. Before I leave, I would like to be received into your church and worship the God you worship. Will you grant this?"

"God will grant it, Mandarin," I replied, my eyes full of tears. In the midst of all this suffering and privation, my God was still working. After years of sowing the seed, He was allowing me to see it bear fruit in the heart of this hon-ored and powerful representative of Old China.

* * *

My mule inn was a complete shambles, but I continued to use the courtyard as a sort of first-aid station.

I had sent most of my children to various Christian homes in the surrounding villages, but I was needed in Yangcheng. Just around the corner from my inn, a family had been com-pletely wiped out; so I used their desolate house as my tem-porary home.

Often as many as forty wounded men—sometimes Japa-nese, sometimes Chinese—would be carried into my court-yard during the day. There were no organized field hospi-tals, and the suffering was terrible. I did what I could for the less severely wounded—put on bandages, gave them food and drink, and let them rest until they were taken off to their various camps. I still had Mr. Lu, the evangelist, with me, and at times there were other Chinese Christians who gave what help they could, but it was shockingly inadequate.

Two days after the Japanese retreated for the second time, a crowd of Chinese women trooped into my battered courtyard. They were bewildered, weary of war and unhappy, and I seized the opportunity of telling them that the great God I served cared for them and could give them peace of heart even in these awful circumstances.

I stood in the middle of the courtyard and held up a large Bible picture. I looked around on them all, my heart full of pity for them because they did not know God's love.

"We are all sinners," I said, pointing unthinkingly at a crowd in the doorway.

"God says all have sinned, and the wages of sin is death. But because God did not want us to perish, He sent His Son, the Lord Jesus Christ, to die on the cross for your sins and mine. If you will believe in Him and accept Him as your Saviour, you will have great peace and happiness in your heart. And even if the enemy comes again and kills your body, your spirit will go to heaven where Jesus is."

Gradually the women drifted away to whatever was left of their homes, and I went inside to try to make up some sort of meal. There was only one small boy, Timothy, and Lu Yung Cheng, a Chinese evangelist, with me, but even finding food for three was a problem.

About half an hour later, Lu Yung Cheng rushed in. "Have you had visitors?" he panted.

"Only the Chinese women who have been unable to come during the occupation."

"No one else?"

"Why do you ask?"

"Because the general is coming here for you."

Almost before he had finished speaking, some soldiers marched in and spoke to Lu Yung Cheng.

"I have to go with these soldiers," he said, looking strangely pale.

"But why do you take him?" I asked the men.

"He is wanted at headquarters."

I could do nothing, and sadly I watched my only companions marched off. I was left alone, wondering what would be the next move. I was not left long in doubt. A few moments later more soldiers marched in. I tried to greet them in a friendly fashion. After all, they were our soldiers, not the Japanese. I went into the kitchen to make tea, but when I came out, I realized that this was certainly not a friendly visit, for the six soldiers stood stiffly on guard all around the courtyard.

"Sit down and have some tea," I invited the one nearest to me, though I felt anything but comfortable.

"Soldiers on duty do not sit down," he replied curtly.

There was nothing I could do but wait and pray that Timothy and Lu Cheng would return soon, and that these men would leave.

Two hours later there was a commotion in the courtyard. I went outside and realized that the general himself had actually deigned to pay me a visit. I bowed to him, and asked him to enter my poor home.

He glared at me fiercely. "Do you know, woman, that you are under arrest?"

"But why?"

He still glared, but made no answer. I turned and went back into the kitchen, my legs feeling very shaky. He followed me in.

"Woman, what do you know about me?"

"Nothing, except that from your uniform I conclude you are the general who has retaken our city and, of course, I have heard your name."

"Who told you about me?"

"Nobody. I only know what everyone else in the city knows."

"Oh, yes, someone did! Tell me who it was, and I will take my soldiers away."

Again and again I declared that I knew nothing of his private life. But he continued to rave and curse and, at length, after much shouting, he left. But the soldiers were still on guard.

A little later I asked them politely if I could send out for some food. They refused, so I ate the small bowl of porridge which was all I had in the house. Still there was no sign of Timothy or Lu Yung Cheng, so I lay down, fully dressed, to get what rest I could.

It was about ten o'clock when there was a great noise outside again.

"Come down, I say, come down at once!" shouted a man's harsh voice.

Getting up, I leaned over the balcony. "I am not one of your soldiers. I am a free citizen of China," I replied with dignity. "You come up here."

Once more the general stamped in, swearing terribly, and stood glaring at me in the broken doorway.

"I demand, for the last time, that you tell me who told you private things about me. If you do, I will see that everything is easy for you."

"I cannot tell you. I do not understand what you mean. I have never seen you before. No one has ever spoken about you."

After more threatenings and cursings, he left again.

For two days I remained under guard without food, for the soldiers would neither send out for any for me nor allow me to go out. On the third day the general, accompanied by more soldiers, marched in and sat down.

"Woman, you have been here three days, are you ready to tell me the name of the person who told you about me?"

"I cannot, for I do not know what you are talking about."

"Then how did you know that I was a sinner?"

"I only know that the Bible says so."

I picked up my Bible, opened it and handed it to him.

He pulled off his hat, threw it down and began to read. When I saw him without his hat, a picture flashed into my mind of the courtyard crowded with Chinese women. Then I remembered that among those in the doorway I had caught a fleeting glimpse of a man!

For an hour he held my Bible while I turned to verse after verse, pointed them out, and let him read them for himself.

What was this Bible? he demanded. What was this gospel I talked about? Who was Jesus Christ?

I explained as patiently as I could while he argued and questioned.

Hour after hour he went on, but gradually he quieted

down. He quit swearing, and a note of great longing came into his voice.

"It is impossible for me to be saved," he said at length.

"With God nothing is impossible."

"I am too wicked!"

"No one is too wicked. Will you kneel down with me and confess to God that you have sinned, but you want to take Jesus Christ as your Saviour?"

Still the battle waged. "What do I get if I believe?" he demanded.

Another two hours went by while the Spirit of God strove for this man's soul and the devil fought to keep him under his domination. Eventually he knelt down of his own accord, humbly confessed his sins and accepted Jesus Christ as his Saviour and Lord.

By this time I was almost fainting with fatigue and hunger. The general got up from his knees, looked at me, then hurried out and ordered his men to bring me food.

He stood by while I ate. Then he burst out, "If I have taken this God, then I have to tell my men about it, don't I?"

"Yes, if you want to be a real Christian."

"I will address my men tomorrow, but I want you to be with me."

With that he left, taking the guards with him. That night I slept peacefully, utterly exhausted with the strain of the evening.

The next morning men arrived and very politely escorted me to the parade ground. The general made me stand on the platform beside him.

"Up to this time we have been a bandit troop," he said after some preliminaries. "I have led you into affrays largely for the sake of killing and looting, and we have always been successful. Now we will cease to be bandits and become honorable soldiers because last night I took Jesus Christ as my God. I find that this Book [waving my Bible aloft] is against dishonesty and wickedness. Now will every man who is willing to join me come out and promise that we will cease to kill or loot for gain, but will serve this true God."

He got down and handed me my Bible. "Will you get me a Bible for my own, Ai-weh-deh?"

"I will send out to the village and find one for you."

I returned home, rejoicing in this man's brave confession, and sent a messenger around the villages until he found a Christian who could give him a Bible. The messenger took it to the general, who thanked him and said, "Tell Ai-weh-deh that I will come as soon as I am free."

I waited, hoping that he would come soon so that we could pray and read together. But the next morning when Timothy, who had been hiding in one of the Christian homes, returned, he said all the soldiers had left the city during the night.

I was bitterly disappointed, for I had thought this man's testimony to the saving grace of our God would be a great witness, both in the city and among the troops.

I heard nothing more of the general, for the situation swayed back and forth for another two years, sometimes one side winning, sometimes the other. My house was in ruins, so I lived not far off in another house, whose owners had been killed. But I continued to use the old courtyard as a primitive dressing station for the wounded. Often as many as forty men were lying on the floor while I did my best with what poor medical supplies I could muster. I washed their wounds, tied them up, and then sent them off to their own camps. One day a batch of wounded soldiers had just gone and I was attempting to clean the place up somewhat, when a dirty ragged beggar hobbled in.

"Do you want to come in and sit down?" I asked.

He sat down on a stone—we had no furniture. He looked desperately ill, and almost starving.

"Bring some warm food," I said to Timothy. The boy hurried off to the place we called home, and a few moments later returned with a bowl of porridge. I went on cleaning up the yard.

"Don't you know me?" the beggar asked as I came near him.

"No, I don't."

"I belong to Jesus."

"When you have had some food you can tell me about Jesus."

"But I still belong to Jesus." This seemed to be the only sensible remark he could make.

After he had eaten his food, I said, "Where are you going?"

"Home."

"Where is home?"

"Here."

"But surely you do not belong to Yangcheng!"

"I belong to Jesus," he repeated again.

Timothy pulled me aside. "Don't you know who he is?"

"He says he belongs to Yangcheng, but I think he is ill in his head."

"He is the general," Timothy whispered.

I turned and stared at the poor, miserable specimen sitting on the cold stone. "What is your name?" I asked gently.

"No name. I belong to Jesus."

That evening I took him home. Timothy and I cared for him and, very slowly, his health improved. Then I took him to the village where I had left my orphans and where I had often gone to hide during the war.

As my beggar grew stronger, I learned more of his story. On the day when he had bravely confessed his faith before the troops, he had waited in vain for the men to come and promise their allegiance to him. That evening, instead of coming to pray with me as he had promised, he was arrested by his own men. They took away his clothes, tied him on a mule, and went off during the night.

For many months they continued as bandits, burning, looting and rioting. They dragged their general with them everywhere, afraid that he would expose them to the government if they let him go. In every possible way they tried to break his faith. He was tortured, starved, kicked and beaten, but still he held out. Fixed in his mind was the knowledge that because he belonged to Jesus Christ he could no longer be a bandit.

Aften nine months of this terrible testing, when they were in the northernmost part of the province, a man came to where he was tied up one night and said, "We did far better when you were our leader. We want you back. Will you lead us again?"

"No, because I must still stand for Jesus Christ."

"Then if you are really sure, I will help you to get away."

Later the man managed to give him a suit of peasant clothes and set him on the way back. He begged in the villages, worked in the fields, always afraid that his men would find him and wreak terrible vengeance on him. In every place, though he knew so little, he told people that he belonged to Jesus Christ and was His servant.

The life he had endured took its toll, however, and he became very ill. Some village women helped him, though by now his mind was very clouded. All he could remember was that he belonged to Jesus and Yangcheng. After fifteen months of wandering, he made his way to Yangcheng, and, instead of a bullying, cursing general, came into the same courtyard as a poor, battered, penniless beggar. This faith implanted that one night of struggle had been as a grain of mustard seed and had remained unmovable, though all else had gone from him.

As his health improved, his mind cleared once more; but the blustering bandit had gone. In the village the children adored him and hung around him. No one except Timothy and myself knew his true identity. To the Christians he was Lao Dah (Big Brother) and they truly loved him. The women gave him little delicacies they made, and the men brought him back *ling tang* (raw sugar) when they returned with their mules, and to them *ling tang* was very precious.

But Lao Dah never really grew strong again. His chest had been weakened by suffering and exposure, and a year after his return, he died. The Christians in the village mourned him with great sorrow—to them he had indeed become Lao Dah.

We never knew his real name, but I was proud to have him buried as Wong-wei-deh, my brother; proud to know that "my son in the faith" had endured so faithfully for our Saviour and Lord.

10

Flight

ALL DURING THE WAR I kept on having children thrust upon me—poor, neglected little waifs whom no one wanted. Every week some new child would be added to my family. Villagers and soldiers brought in orphans, and sometimes children walked in on their own, for they were told that Ai-weh-deh would care for them.

As the war dragged on year after year, the numbers grew until we had over a hundred children to care for, and some of them were by no means perfect angels. Like all normal youngsters, they were naughty, they needed constant attention, and they needed feeding.

I tried to give them lessons, to teach them psalms and something of the Bible. The general to whom I gave my information about the enemy, and many others, became interested in my work.

"I hear, Ai-weh-deh, that you are looking after a hundred or more children in the ruins of your mission," the general said one day. "What do you do when the Japanese occupy the town? How do you get food for such a large family?"

"When the Japanese take the town, we carry on just the same. When they bomb we go out into the caves in the mountains, and come back when it is over. We use the hall as a dressing station just the same, and often we have your men and the Japanese in at the same time. I beg food from everybody—the Japanese as well as anyone else. We have always managed, for God always provides."

"Have you heard of the orphanages that Madame Chiang has opened for children such as yours, Ai-weh-deh? She has government money, and all over China, temples and colleges are being requisitioned to house homeless children. I suggest that you write to her and tell her what you are doing and ask her help."

I wrote that letter and the reply came back: "If you can bring the children into Free China to Shensi, we will look after them. I will also send you money for your work in Yangcheng if someone can collect it."

We discussed the matter with the elders of the mission hall and decided that Mr. Lu, the evangelist, should take down the first party of children and collect the money in Shensi. It was a hard, difficult journey, for it meant walking for days over the mountains, crossing the Yellow River, and then going still farther west. Mr. Lu agreed to go, and the children were wildly excited.

They set off eventually, about a hundred of them, taking provisions for a day or two. They would have to beg or buy more on the way. We expected the journey to take about two weeks, so that Mr. Lu would be back within the month.

After they left, things went on as before. Children kept coming in greater numbers; we had a hundred again before the month was up. My Chinese helpers and I went on with our teaching, our story telling, and our efforts to keep them clean and with enough to eat. We waited for Mr. Lu, but one month passed, then two, and he did not appear, nor was there any news.

The war situation had become steadily worse. One day the general's wife told me in great confidence that the Chinese army was about to retreat. "You must come with us, Ai-weh-deh," she said. "We will look after you and the children, and you will be safe with us."

I thought and prayed about it. Then I said, "You take the children, but I must stay. Christians never retreat."

That night an officer called with a letter from the general himself, begging me to accompany them. On the back of the letter I wrote, "Christians never retreat."

The next day this party of children also left us, and the mission hall was deserted; but I had decided my place was here. The Japanese had come before, and I had lived through it, so they could come again.

Two nights after the children left, I was preparing for bed. I had read my Bible, said my prayers, and was just climbing into bed when there was a knock at the door.

"Who is there?" I demanded.

It was a soldier and a member of our mission hall. So throwing on my gown again, I let him in.

"Ai-weh-deh, you must retreat with us," he broke out.

"No, I won't. My place is here. I have work to do."

"I have been sent by the general to plead with you to

change your mind. Even if you do not retreat with us, Ai-weh-deh, you must leave Yangcheng."

"But why?"

"The Japanese intend to take the city tonight or tomorrow and they want certain people."

"That has nothing to do with me. I will stay as I have done before."

"But you are one of the people they want."

"Me? What do they want with me? No, you are just saying this to make me leave."

"Then look at this." And from his pocket he pulled a crude poster. "I found this on the city wall. They are all over the place."

I stared at it. "Wanted: Ai-weh-deh" was printed on it, together with three other names. "Any person giving information which will lead to the capture, alive or dead, of the above mentioned, will receive a reward of £100 from the Japanese High Command."

"I must think this over," I said slowly. "Thank the general and all of you. Good-bye."

He left, and I sat on alone, not knowing what to do. Then, late as it was, I went to the mission hall and consulted an elder.

"You must go, Ai-weh-deh, you must go," he said firmly.

The women who were there wept. "Oh, don't leave us; you are our mother, don't leave us."

I went back to my room, my mind in a turmoil. I burned all my papers and photographs, but I still did not know what to do. I did not want to throw my life away for nothing, and I knew the Japanese would have no mercy on a "wanted person." But did God want me to stay with my people and help them? I got out my Bible and prayed and prayed, "O Lord, tell me what to do. I'm all mixed up. I don't know if I should go or stay; please tell me."

I opened my Bible, and the first words I read were "Flee ye; flee ye into the mountains; dwell deeply in hidden places, because the king of Babylon has conceived a purpose against you."

That was enough for me. I had no more doubts; I would leave the next day. I went to bed and slept peacefully. Early in the morning I was up and ready to be off. I called to the gateman, "Get my mule ready, and take me down the road."

"No mule will get out of here today, Ai-weh-deh. They are here; they came last night. Come and look."

I looked through a peephole in the gate, and there, on the roadside, sat the Japanese soldiers washing their feet.

"Let me out of the other gate, then," I said. This was the gate through which the Chinese carried the dead, but that did not matter now. Unless I got out at once, I also was as good as dead. I had only one thought now, and that was to run—run—run, as far away as possible.

I got through the Gate of the Dead, across a stream, and started to run across a field. Then the Japanese saw me. Bullets splattered all around, and there was a great deal of shouting. I fell down. The bullets came closer. I pulled off my thick padded coat, and rolled under a bush. The bullets riddled my coat, but eventually I crawled out and ran on again. I fell, got up, ran, crawled and climbed, but eventually the firing ceased, and I sank down utterly exhausted. After a while, I set off again and made for a road. I walked all day, and at night reached a friendly village where I was welcomed and given refreshment.

The next morning I set off again, and in the evening reached Cheng Tsuen where many of my children were.

11

The Long Trek

ON MY WAY I had decided that I would take the children myself to Shensi. It was impossible to keep these children in the war zone any longer, and by now I knew that something must have happened to Mr. Lu.

It was not until long afterward that I learned that he had gotten through safely with his crowd of children, and was on his way back when he was arrested and brought before a military court. Because his dialect was that of Tsincheng, which was occupied by the enemy, the authorities refused to believe his story about the children, but locked him up as a suspected Japanese spy.

My friends tried to dissuade me. "It is miles and miles to Sian, and you have no food and no money with which to transport a hundred children. You might stand a chance of getting through alone, but not with such a crowd of little ones," they said.

"The Lord will provide," I replied. "I believe these

children must go to Shensi, and there is no one else to take
them. Tell the big children to get the little ones ready, and
say we are going for a nice, long walk."

"But which way will you go? The Japanese control every
road."

"Then we must go over the mountains and down to the
Yellow River."

"Go over the mountains with all these children? You must
be mad!"

"They are not safe here. Any day they may be bombed and
killed. There is danger for them everywhere until they are in
Free China."

I went to the mayor and begged grain for the journey. After a great deal of argument he said, "I will give you enough
to last until the next town, Ai-weh-deh, and two men to
carry it for you. I admire your courage, but it is very fool-
ish."

Early the next morning, we set off—one hundred children
whose ages ranged from under three to sixteen.

At first some of the children ran excitedly in front, some
dawdled by the way, and some dashed here and there. But
as the day wore on, they quieted down and were glad to keep
to the road. The big ones helped the little ones along, often
carrying them on their backs.

The two men stayed with us that first day, then I recruited
two from another village the next day. The people of the
towns and villages helped us if they could, but food was
scarce.

Often there was no proper road, only a mule track, and we
walked on and on, over the mountain ranges. We slept by the

roadside or in temples. Once we spent the night in a soldiers' camp, but usually we lay down where we were under the open sky. We had no blankets, so we slept in tight clusters to keep each other warm. We begged food all along the way, but often all we had for supper was thin gruel. As the days passed, the children became fretful and showed signs of exhaustion, and there were many tears.

"Ai-weh-deh, my feet hurt!" "My shoes are worn clear through!" "Ai-weh-deh, my tummy aches. I cannot walk anymore." The older children grew too tired to carry the little ones, and our marches grew shorter and shorter.

I tried everything I could think of to distract their attention from their aches and pains and to keep them trudging on. We would sing all the hymns and choruses we knew. Sometimes I would start a text like "Bless the Lord, O my soul," and the children would reply, "And all that is within me, bless His holy name." Or I would say, "Jesus Christ came into the world" and they would shout, "to save sinners!" It used to bring a lump to my throat and tears to my eyes to hear the poor little mites sing "Count your blessings" when, at present, they had so few blessings to count.

For twelve long, weary days and twelve shivering nights we struggled on and on. How far is it to the Yellow River? How many more days must we walk? How many more mountains must we cross? were the first questions when we reached a village.

Then, at last, we climbed the last range of mountains, and there before us we saw gleaming in the sun—like a beckoning ribbon of gold—the Yellow River!

"See, there is Yuen Chu!" the older children called to the

little ones. "When we get there we will have plenty of food, and we will be able to paddle and swim."

But the little town of Yuen Chu, that lay near the banks of the river, was deserted. Every house was empty. There was no food, and the children wept bitterly with disappointment.

At last I found a few soldiers. "Can you please give us some food?" I pleaded.

"How many of you are there?"

"A hundred children."

"It is impossible to feed so many. We have rations only for three days for ourselves. We will give you a little, but for one hundred!"

"Is there any food in the town?"

"Not a scrap! Everyone has been evacuated. The Japanese are expected any day. Our army has retreated across the river, and there is nothing left for the enemy."

We made some thin soup and ate it by the roadside, then I led my dispirited, disappointed, weary band down to the riverside, near the ferry.

"If we stay here we will get the first boat across tomorrow morning," I said as cheerfully as I could. We bathed our tired feet and laid down on the riverbanks to sleep, but the children were awake long before dawn.

"We are so hungry, Ai-weh-deh. Is there no food for us?" they cried.

"We'll soon be over the river, and there is plenty of food there. The boats will be here before long."

We waited, straining our eyes to the other shore. But long after it was light, there was still no sign of movement. I realized then that ferry boats had ceased to run; but I did not tell the children, though the big ones soon guessed for themselves.

Finally I called six of the older boys. "We will go back into the town and see if we can find something. The rest of you must stay here in case the boat comes."

We walked to the military headquarters where I asked the captain, "Are there any boats going across the river today?"

"The river is closed. There will be no boats going across because they are all at the other side."

"But what about the ferry?"

"That is closed too. We can do nothing. The Japanese are expected any hour now."

I went down on my knees and begged for food for my children, but they would give me none. I went to another military post and begged again. They would hardly believe that what I told them was true.

"Where have you come from?"

"We have walked from Yangcheng over the mountains. It has been a terrible journey."

"We will give you a little food, but we have only enough for the smallest children. We cannot possibly feed you all."

I was almost in despair. All night I worried and prayed, prayed and worried. I was at the end of my tether.

If only I wasn't saddled with all these children, I thought bitterly. *Nobody else bothered about them, why did I have to get myself and them into this mess?*

Then a voice said, "I died for these children. I loved every one of them. I gave them to you to look after, for My sake."

So the hours went by until the dawn broke. A girl of thirteen, called Sualan, stood beside me. "Ai-weh-deh, do you

remember when God called Moses that he took the children
of Israel through the Red Sea on dry land and every one of
them got safely across?"

I nodded. Sualan smiled sweetly at me as she asked, "Do
you believe it?"

"Of course, I do!" I replied immediately. "I would not
teach you anything I did not believe."

"Then why don't *we* go across?" she asked simply.

That shook me. "But I am not Moses," I gasped.

"Of course you are not, but Jehovah is still God!"

That was like a physical blow. All the years I had been
preaching had I really believed that Moses did take the children of Israel through the Red Sea? Did I believe that the
waters rolled back, and stood up on either side while they
crossed dry-shod? I had staked my life on God's mighty
power. Why did I doubt now?

I turned to Sualan. "We will go across," I said, and truly
I believed it. Sualan called some of the older ones together
and we knelt in prayer. Sualan prayed simply, "Here we are,
Lord, just waiting for You to open the Yellow River for us."

For myself, I bowed in silence, but in my heart I said, "O
God, I am finished. I can do nothing more. I am at the end.
I am nothing. It is only You, Lord, now—You above! O
God, don't let us down. Save us—prove Yourself."

Some of the little boys ran up and pulled my skirt. "Get
up, get up!" they shouted. "There is a big man here!"

I was trembling all over when I stood up. A Chinese officer stood watching me.

"Are you in charge of these children?" he asked.

"Yes."

"How many are here?"

"A hundred."

"What are you doing here?"

"Waiting to cross the river."

"But who are you?"

"I am Ai-weh-deh, of the mission hall in Yangcheng."

"Are you crazy? Do you not realize that we expect a Japanese infantry attack at any moment? Don't you know that Japanese aircraft are patrolling all the time? If they spot these children they will machine-gun them. Who are these children, anyway?"

"We are refugees trying to reach Sian."

"Refugees! Then why did you not cross the river long ago?"

"We could not get a boat."

"You did not expect us to leave boats for the Japanese, did you? But I will signal for one now."

He made a long, low whistle, like a seabird, "Oo—oo—oo!" and raised his arm.

"The boat will be across at once. There is a village on the other side where you can get food."

"Oh, thank you!"

"Are you looking after these children alone?"

"Yes."

"But surely you are a foreigner?"

"Yes."

"You have chosen a strange occupation."

He had hardly finished speaking when the children cried out excitedly that the boat was coming. The first lot got in, and the boat went backward and forward until all were safely over.

The people of the town took the children into their homes and fed them until they could eat no more. Then the children talked, telling of their terrible journey over the mountains.

"All of us bigger ones helped to carry the little ones," they boasted. "And Ai-weh-deh was always carrying one or two of the sick ones. And when we got to the river we waited and waited for a boat. We prayed for the river to be opened so that we could walk across like the children of Israel did, across the Red Sea, but God knew we were so tired of walking so He sent a boat, and that was far better."

After a few days' rest, we set off again to Mienchin where we could get a train that would take us within a few days' march of Sian.

The children had never seen a train before. At the first puff of the engine and the blast of its whistle, there was a great scream of terror, and every child disappeared. They were dragged from under carts, out of barrels, from behind doors and, with difficulty, persuaded to climb on board.

At Shanchow the train stopped. A porter shouted, "All change—all change. The train is not going any farther, you must get out."

"But there are lines ahead; I can see them," I argued.

"Listen, woman," he said impatiently, "those lines go close to the river. The Japanese are on the other side, and where the river is narrow they shoot across. Understand?"

"But what can we do?"

"You walk from here. You see those mountains? You

cross them and go down the other side. Then you can rejoin the train."

"But those mountains are thousands of feet high, and we have babies with us. We are already tired out. How can we get across?"

"How do I know? You had better see the stationmaster."

I pleaded with the stationmaster. "Please, sir, can't you help us? I have a hundred weary children with me. We have been on the road twenty days already. The children cannot get over those mountains."

"I am sorry but there is nothing we can do. This train goes no farther, so you must all get out. There is a hut over there where you can spend the night, and the refugee people will give you food."

"Oh, please sir, there must be something you can do to help us to reach Sian."

"Madam, there are millions of refugees all over China."

"But these are children!"

"Madam, I can do nothing more. If you wish to go farther, the only way is across those mountains. I will send two soldiers with you. There is only one pass left open. The Japanese are on the one side and our troops on the other, but the soldiers will help you to get through."

"How long will it take?"

"If you start early in the morning, you should reach Tungkwan in two days."

I looked at the mountains, the tops of which were hidden by the clouds. As far as I could make out there was only a faint mule track.

"Thank you very much," I said. "If there is no other way, we must attempt it. We will be ready to start at dawn."

I had no sleep that night. The journey before me was going to try even the strongest, and some of the children already were ill. But what could I do? We could not go back, and we could not stay here. I had to get the children to safety whatever it cost me.

The journey was far worse than any we had undertaken. The mountain tracks were steep and in many places had fallen away. We had to scramble over loose rocks and slide down steep slopes. It was a nightmare journey and, without the help of the soldiers, many of the children would never have gotten through. We had to watch them continually as they slipped here and there. The soldiers and I had to carry one, or sometimes two, children apiece all the way, and constantly urge the others forward.

We slept on the bare mountain and then trudged onward for another long day. In the evening we reached Tungkwan and cheered up at the sight of the railway station. The officials, however, shook their heads. "There are no more trains from here; it is too dangerous."

"But what can we do?" I cried in desperation. "We have come over the mountains from Sanchow and before that we had walked for twenty days from Yangcheng. We are going to Free China to Madame Chiang's orphanages. They were expecting us. Is there nothing you can do? My children cannot walk any farther; many of them are ill."

"If I help you, are you willing to obey my instructions implicitly?"

"Yes, if it means getting the children through."

"Are you willing to travel at your own risk?"

"Yes, oh, yes!"

"Then I will tell you in confidence. One train does go through. Every morning before dawn, a coal train goes through to Hua Shan. Sometimes where the river is narrow the Japanese shoot at it, sometimes not. If they heard voices or saw people, they would certainly shoot. Can you promise to keep your children quiet?"

"Oh, yes. I will see that they do not move or make a sound."

"Tomorrow before dawn, then, you will find the coal trucks waiting here. Get aboard. But if you value your lives, keep your heads down. And good luck, lady! I admire your courage."

We lay down in the fields, and when the little ones were asleep I called Sualan and the other older boys and girls together.

"Listen carefully," I said. "All of you are old enough to understand that tonight you must keep the little ones absolutely quiet. If they make a noise, the Japanese will shoot at us. You must go to sleep for a little while, but when I wake you, you must carry all the little ones and place them between big lumps of coal on top of the truck."

"But what will we do if they waken?"

"They are so worn out that they will not awaken if you are careful. When they do awaken we will be out of danger. You understand?"

"Yes, Ai-weh-deh."

"Go, then, and sleep now. I will wake you when it is time to go."

"But will you not sleep yourself, Ai-weh-deh?"

"Perhaps I shall doze," I replied.

"But you are ill, Ai-weh-deh; you should rest. For days you have been ill. You have carried one child, sometimes two, all day, and you have given nearly all the food to us."

"The Lord will help me to carry on. I will rest when we get to Sian. Now you must go to sleep."

I lay down on the bare ground, every bone in my body aching, but my heart was touched at the love and sympathy the children felt for me.

"Please, God, give me strength to take them where they will be cared for," I prayed. "Help us all to reach Sian."

After a few hours I awakened the older ones and, in silence, we carried the younger children, one by one, and placed them gently on top of the coal. The hard lumps did not disturb them, for they had slept out for many nights now, and they were utterly exhausted with their trek of the last two days.

The train moved off and I lay tensed, but not a shot was fired. When the little ones finally awoke, they screamed with laughter at the sight of each other covered with coal dust.

"You have gone black in the night," they laughed. And with the quick recovery of childhood they were as lively as crickets for a little while.

Once more we had to leave the train and, with clothes in a filthy condition, we set out on the last walk—just three days to Sian, we were told! We begged food from soldiers and villagers; we slept on the roadside, and we kept on trying to sing until at long last Sian, which stood for us almost as the Celestial City, lay before us.

Our weary feet hurried forward, but we were rudely halted.

The city gates were closed and, though I pleaded, the gate-keeper refused to open them.

"You cannot come in here," he shouted. "The city gates are closed against refugees. The place is swarming with them already. There is no food—nothing. You must go somewhere else."

"But there is money waiting for us here. We have been on the road for twenty-seven days. We were told to come here. You must let us in, you must!"

This last disappointment was too much for me. We trailed around the city walls, but every gate was closed. What could I do? Where could we go?

Then someone took pity on us and told me of a Buddhist temple at Fu-Feng, where children were cared for. It was only a day's train journey away, and it was one of Madame Chiang's orphanages.

By now I was too ill to remember much of what happened. We must have gone on the train, for when we reached the orphanage, food and beds were ready for us. My children were safe at last! My work for them was finished.

The next morning I called the children together and said, "Let us say thank you to God for all His love to us." We said "The Lord is my Shepherd" together, then I said good-bye to them.

The people at the orphanage begged me to stay and rest until I was well again, but my mind was in a turmoil. I could not rest; I had to go on. There was so much I had to do. "God will care for me," I kept repeating, and set out to preach in the villages.

I do not remember what happened after that until I found

myself in a hospital in Sian. Gradually I learned what had happened.

I had tried to preach in a village, but had collapsed. No one knew who I was, so a boy went to the American missionary who got a cow cart and took me to the mission house. After two days they had brought a doctor from the Sian hospital. He had shaken his head over me. "There is very little hope; she has pneumonia and typhus. Do you know who she is?"

"Not the vaguest idea. She has not spoken a word since we brought her here."

"If we could get her to the hospital, there is a chance we might save her. It is a long journey, but if we could get a cattle truck put onto the midnight train we could take her as she is, in this bed."

I was taken in that cattle truck, and learned that kind, unknown friends knelt around the bed to hold it steady during the journey. They scarcely dared to hope I would be alive when we reached Sian. Suddenly, to their amazement, I began to sing a hymn; then I prayed and preached a sermon on the prodigal son. They could not understand all I said for my dialect was of the north, but they still believed I was Chinese.

In the hospital at Sian, they fought to save me.

"She should have been dead long ago," the doctor said. "She is suffering from relapsing fever, typhus, pneumonia, malnutrition, utter exhaustion and probably many other minor complaints."

I was too ill to talk, and for over a month I lay in the hospital, conscious of very little that went on around me.

Then, like a miracle, our own Mr. Lu from Yangcheng arrived in Sian. He had been released and had set out immediately to try to find the other batch of children and myself.

The Chinese pastor brought Mr. Lu to visit me, and he was overjoyed to find I was still alive.

"She is from Yangcheng in north China," he told the doctor and nurses.

"Then what is she doing here, in Sian? It is hundreds of miles away."

"She has been bringing children to safety from behind the Japanese lines."

"What is her name?"

"I only know her Chinese name, Ai-weh-deh, but there is a boy whom she brought from Yangcheng, and he has a book that belonged to her. He carried it all the way in his pocket. It is an English book, and it has some writing in it."

They eventually found the book, and on the flyleaf was written, "To Gladys from Aunt Bessie."

They stared at me in amazement. Was it possible that I was not Chinese as they imagined?

12

The Stethoscope

I HAVE NO IDEA how long I lay in that Baptist hospital, for typhus affected my memory, and the following two years are very hazy.

I know I was a wreck physically when the hospital authorities finally decided they could do no more for me, and mentally I must have been in an even worse state.

I could not walk, but Mr. and Mrs. Fisher took me to their home in the little mission station at Mei Shein. And if I remember little else, I remember how lovingly they cared for me. Mrs. Fisher was a trained nurse and gradually helped me back to a certain measure of health, at least physically.

When I left their house I stayed for several months in the mission owned by the national church at Fu Feng because my children were in the orphanage there, and I could see them and they could visit me. I went out preaching in the villages; but because my children longed to have a home once more with me, I moved back to Sian.

Chang Tsi Ni, a Chinese evangelist, had once run a factory to employ poor Christians; but now he was old and ill, and the factory was standing empty.

It was in a room at the back of this factory that I went to live with fourteen of my children. Some of these were now growing up and able to help a little. When the girls reached the age of twelve they brought sewing and mending home and were paid so much for a set amount. The boys, as soon as they could, went out each day and carried loads or did other odd jobs. The little money they brought in was a great help at this time.

It was in connection with one of these boys that I had a wonderful experience concerning answered prayer.

Chu En was the son of a Chinese pastor who had been killed by the Japanese. His mother was trying to escape with her five children when she was taken seriously ill on the riverbank at Yangcheng. I was asked to visit her, but it was too late to do anything. She died the next day and we had the five orphans left on our hands.

I adopted Chu En, and the other four were taken in by different Chinese Christian families. Chu En was always a quiet, studious boy, obviously very intelligent, and I never had any trouble with him. He was with me two or three years before we took that awful journey over the mountains to Sian, but by that time he was the only one of his family still alive. One sister had died of tuberculosis, two other children were killed during the raids, and his younger brother had joined what was called the "Children's Army," which was simply wiped out in a terrible slaughter by the enemy.

It was perhaps these awful experiences which had made

Chu En serious and thoughtful beyond his years. I knew he ought to go to school and continue his education, but I had no money to keep my large family.

Then a Dr. Tsung noticed Chu En, on a visit to Sian, and suggested that I should let him take the boy home with him and he would help him in his studies. Gladly I accepted the offer, and Chu En accompanied Dr. Tsung to his home on the borders of Yenan.

It was almost a year later when he returned for the New Year holiday—the one great celebration time in China.

He had grown taller, was even more serious and polite, and I was proud to call him "my son."

The night before Chu En was due to return to Dr. Tsung's home, he startled me by announcing calmly that as soon as possible he was going to return to Yangcheng.

"Oh, no, you are not, Chu En," I said emphatically. "You cannot go back. All that we knew and loved there has been destroyed; that is not home to us anymore. Yangcheng is wholly occupied by the enemy, and there is no way back."

I thought that had settled the matter, and the next day Chu En returned to Dr. Tsung.

Three months later, as I was preparing for bed one night, I heard someone moving about outside my room. I opened the door and called, "Who is there?"

"Me. Chu En."

"Chu En! Why are you here? Are you in trouble? Have you run away?"

"Oh, no, nothing is wrong, but I am going home."

"Chu En, we settled all that when you were here at New Year's."

"You settled it, Ma. It was you who talked. If you remember, I said nothing."

"Maybe that is so, but it does not alter the fact that you cannot go."

"Ma, do you remember what you felt like when you knew God wanted you to come to China?"

"Of course, but you can know nothing of that."

"I do, because God has spoken to me in the same way. He has told me I must go back to Yangcheng. He has work for me there."

I could not doubt him; all that was left was for me to help and pray. I prayed for a pair of trousers and a pair of shoes. What Chu En prayed for I discovered later.

The days went past, and I wondered why God had not heard me. No trousers, shoes or material came our way.

About ten days later, Chu En said, "Ma, why do you worry about things I do not need? Will you pray for what I really want?"

"But you need shoes and decent trousers."

"I came from Yangcheng without shoes. I can go back the same way. These trousers will cover me a while longer."

"Then what is it you want me to pray for?"

"A stethoscope."

"A stethoscope! What on earth is that?"

"One of those instruments with two things you put in your ears and listen to people's insides with the other end."

"But where could I get a thing like that?"

Chu En shook his head. "I don't know, but God does."

So we prayed for what I believed was almost an impossibility—a stethoscope.

Another week passed by. Then one day in the street I met an old refugee woman whom I thought I had seen in church the previous day.

I stopped and spoke to her. "Did I see you in the refugee church on Sunday?"

"Oh, yes, I was there."

"Where do you come from?"

"My pot of food is on the fire; come to my hut while we talk."

Turning, we went into a small hut, and I sat on the stool while she stirred her pot on the fire.

As my eyes grew accustomed to the dim light, I looked around. There was little to see except a rather unusual red wooden box in one corner.

"You are looking at my box. I brought that all the way from Su Chow. I carried it on my shoulder; it is very, very precious."

"What is in it?"

"How should I know? I have not opened it."

"Then how do you know it is precious?"

"Because it belonged to our nice clean lady."

"Who was she?"

"A lady who came to our village and told us about Jesus. Oh, she was lovely, so clean and kind. The enemy was coming, but the men of our village were determined they would not harm our nice lady. So they carried her to a cave and hid her, but she left her box behind in my house. Before she could return we had to flee. But I could not leave my dear lady's box for the enemy, so I carried it safely all the way."

"Will you let me open the box?"

"Certainly not. Who are you that it should have anything to do with you? Are you a relative of hers?"

"Yes."

"What relation?"

"Her fifth cousin." This was the relationship that all Chinese of the same name claim with each other.

She stared at me closely. "Yes, you are rather like her."

I nodded. "We are all alike; we all do the same thing because we belong to the same country."

"Very well, then, you may open the box."

Inside that box was a queer collection—food that had gone bad, odds and ends of clothes, a few books, and at the bottom a small leather case.

I opened this case and could scarcely believe my eyes. On one flap lay a thermometer, tweezers, scissors and, in the bottom, a stethoscope!

Picking out the answer to our prayer with hands that trembled, I said, "Will you let me take this away? Later I will return and decide what to do with these other things."

She stared at the queer object in my hand, then nodded her head.

"You are my lady's relative. If that strange thing is of use to you, take it; it is of no use to anyone here."

Jubilantly I hurried home, and waved the stethoscope when I saw Chu En in the courtyard.

"God has answered our prayers."

Chu En seized the stethoscope and hugged it to him as he said, "Now do you believe God wants me to go back to Yangcheng?"

The next day, still wearing his old trousers and with no

shoes on his feet, no food or money, only the precious stethoscope in a little bundle, Chu En set off. I have never seen him since.

Three months later I received a scrap of paper: "I am well, are you well? Praise the Lord, hallelujah." No name or address, but I recognized the writing as Chu En's.

Three months later I had an identical note. Then the Communists took Shansi, and there was silence. I thought Chu En, like so many more, had given his life for his faith.

About eighteen months later I met a man who spoke in the dialect of Yangcheng. He asked me to tell him the gospel.

"Why do you ask?"

"All I know is that if you have this gospel you have peace and joy in your heart."

"But how do you know that?"

"Where I come from I have watched nine people being baptized in the river. When I asked how they had courage to do this when it was forbidden by the Communists, they said it was because they had Christ in their hearts."

"But how did they know of baptism if no one is preaching?"

"Because there is a wise young man, who has a curious instrument with which he listens and knows all that goes on inside. He has told them about Jesus."

So Chu En was still giving the water of life to needy souls in spite of enemy opposition. Yangcheng—the place so dear to my heart—still had its witness. Someday Chu En will tell me the whole story of the stethoscope and how it helped him during those awful days.

13

The God Who Loves

REFUGEES FROM THE EAST came pouring into Sian speaking completely different dialects. Among them were three godly Christians from Shansi, Mr. and Mrs. Wong and Mr. Cheng.

These three and myself decided that something must be done, so we obtained permission to use the disused factory belonging to Chang Tsi Ni as a church in which we could preach in an understandable dialect for these refugees from Hopeh, Honan, Shantung, etc.

We called it the Independent Christian Church, but we were certainly not isolated. Near us was the Baptist Church with George Young as its pastor, and the Church of England with Bishop Sheng as its vicar, and our three churches were in perfect unison. We were one in spirit, in purpose and in desire—nothing but true service to God and blessing for the needy souls around us. We might have had different names, but we were surely "all one in Christ Jesus."

If a refugee went to the Baptist Church or the Church of England and it was felt that maybe we would be able to help them more easily, then he was escorted to us and introduced. If one church had a convention then the members of the other two attended and were blessed.

After a time I left most of the children in the care of Pastor Ma, as I was unable to care for them and be out preaching continually at the same time.

I was still far from fully recovered, and again I have much for which to thank kind friends. Mr. and Mrs. Young, Miss Major, the hospital matron, and Bishop Sheng, together with the children, especially Ninepence, cared for me and prayed for me continually.

Often I was forgetful and careless about many things; only in the matter of the gospel was my mind utterly clear. Maybe it is to Bishop Sheng more than anyone that I owe my restoration to a more normal state. Though little older than myself, he talked to me like a father and gradually made me take a firmer grip upon the normal circumstances of everyday life.

Eventually the Japanese, who had overrun Shansi, were reported to be on their way to Shensi, so we fled from Sian to Boa Chi. A short while before this had been a small village; then with the influx of refugees it had grown like a mushroom into a huge city. From here I went to Fenghsien to Mr. and Mrs. Fisher again, and with them worked among the refugees and in the surrounding villages.

While there I was invited to take part in a conference of young people and speak to them about pioneer work. When I arrived at their headquarters I discovered that this group was actually from Kai Feng. They had been students in the school there but had been driven out by the enemy. Many of the students had scattered, but about sixty of them had determined to keep together and study when they could. They had carried along with them benches and books and various other things from the college, and had studied while they trekked. Now they had reached Fenghsien.

I did not give the lectures because I became ill again. I lay in bed, weak and full of doubts. Why had God allowed me to come here among strangers, all for nothing? One day I heard murmurs coming from the next room. It sounded as if people were praying.

I crept out of bed, threw on my outer garment and slippers, and slipped out to investigate. Peeping in the open doorway I saw about fifteen students squatting around what was obviously a map.

Then one went forward, shut his eyes and poked with his finger at the map, much as I had often done as a child when we had played the game of putting on the donkey's tail. When he opened his eyes, he read aloud the name of the place where his finger had landed, and said, "Does anyone know anything about this place?"

I stood entranced while one after another prayed about this unknown town or village. Then another went forward, again jabbed blindly with his finger, and read another name.

At the end of the meeting, I questioned the students and learned that they had this part of the northwest laid on their hearts and were praying for different places every day.

For three weeks I stayed there, in bed most of the time.

Then at another of these strange prayer meetings I said, "Is anyone going to these places you are praying for?"

"Nobody is free. We have not finished our studies. We have no money and no one knows the country, but now our special prayer is for someone to go and spy out the land."

Two days later I was convinced that God was asking me to go to this unknown territory. I offered myself to this group of earnest, loving young Christians and, with their prayers and blessings ringing in my ears, I set off a few days later .

The countryside was beautiful and for the first few days my leisurely journey was very pleasant. I could converse with those I met, but I knew before long the language would prove a difficulty.

As I went farther into the northwest I managed each morning to get someone to escort me as my guide from his village to the next until I came to Tsin Tsui. I stayed a night or two with friendly Christian people; but when I asked about the road ahead, with one accord everyone advised me to turn back. "You cannot go further," they declared, "this is the end. Further on there is nothing."

"But the world doesn't just end like that," I argued. "I must go on. It is what I have come for."

The villagers shook their heads dolefully. They were sure by now that I must be a little strange. Then, seeing I was fully determined to go forward, a Chinese doctor offered to accompany me for five days. His name was Dr. Huang, and he had always been curious as to what lay outside his immediate district.

Dr. Huang was a Christian, though maybe up to that time

not very deeply taught. But he could read and, as we traveled, we talked and sometimes argued. When I could not convince him, I handed him my Bible and he could read the passage in question for himself.

The five days lengthened to nine. We went on and on, speaking to all whom we met, but not one of them had heard of Jesus Christ, the Son of the God in heaven.

On the tenth day we came out onto a mountainside and that night had to stay in a filthy hut. The next day we plodded on all day but did not meet a living soul or see the slightest sign of human habitation anywhere.

By midafternoon I was becoming perturbed. Where were we going to sleep? Where would we get any food? I was here alone with a man I knew very little about, and I needed company.

I stared around and then burst out, "Dr. Huang, we are going to put down our bundles and pray."

We threw our bundles on the ground and knelt down. "Dear God," I began, "have mercy on us. You can see what a plight we are in. Give us food and shelter for the night."

My whole prayer was taken up by my own wants, my own immediate requirements.

Then very calmly Dr. Huang began to pray. "O God, send us the one You want us to tell about Jesus. We have witnessed to no one today, but You have sent us here for some special purpose. Show us where to find the man You intend to bless."

I felt humbled and ashamed. While I had been so concerned with my own comfort, this man was concerned only with His Father's business.

After a few moments I said, "Shall we sing a chorus?"

So we sat and sang, and our voices must have carried far in the clear mountain air.

Suddenly Dr. Huang jumped to his feet. "There is our man," he cried. And before I could stop him, he had dashed off.

I sat alone, feeling very small and frail in this lonely barren country. Finally I saw two little specks on the mountainside. As he drew nearer, Dr. Huang kept shouting, "Come on up; I have found our man." But I sat stolidly on. To me there seemed no sense in scrambling up that steep, rock-strewn hillside.

Eventually Dr. Huang reached me and said, "God obviously means us to go up, so come along."

"But what about our bundles?"

"Leave them. There is no one here to steal them."

Half carried and half pushed, I scrambled up and found, leaning against a rock, a Tibetan lama priest. I stared from him to Dr. Huang. I knew that lamas were supposed to have nothing to do with women, also that outwardly they appeared to be holy men, but inwardly many of them were bad, immoral, ignorant and superstitious.

"Did you tell him I was a woman?" I demanded of Dr. Huang.

"Yes, but he invited you to come to spend the night in the lamasery."

I hesitated. What were we letting ourselves in for? Why should Tibetan priests invite *me* into their sacred buildings?

"There is nowhere else for us to go," Dr. Huang pointed out.

Suddenly the man spoke and, although his accent was strange, I could understand what he said.

"We have waited long for you to tell us about the God who loves."

My heart jumped and, without another word, we followed our guide up the path. Then we reached the lamasery and I caught my breath at the beauty of the scene. The side of the mountain which we had climbed was barren, yellow and rocky; but on this side, because there was water, the mountain was covered in rich green grass and lovely flowering vines. And at the top stood the lamasery, imposing and stately.

As we approached, my fears returned. The huge gate closed as we went in, and I thought, *we are in, but will we ever get out again?*

A party of lamas greeted us almost reverently and escorted me to a small room. Then men padded backward and forward, bringing everything they could think of for my comfort—tiger rugs, cushions, water for washing, and dish after dish of daintily prepared food. It seemed like a dream!

After our strenuous climb, I felt very weary; I had just decided I would lie down to rest when two men knocked at the door and politely requested me to accompany them. I was joined by Dr. Huang and we were escorted through one courtyard after another until we came to a very large one. In this were five hundred hassocks made of coconut leaves ranged in a rough semicircle, and on each of these hassocks sat a lama with his hands piously crossed and his head bent.

We were taken to two empty hassocks in the center, and sat down. *What on earth are we expected to do?* I wondered nervously.

Dr. Huang said, "Now we will begin. You sing."

"But what shall I sing?"

"Anything."

So in a very trembling voice I sang in Chinese the American chorus "Glorious Freedom."

A deathly silence followed. Then Dr. Huang began to talk. He told them about the Baby who was born in a stable in Bethlehem; then he told them of the Saviour who died on Calvary.

"Now sing again," he said. So I sang, then I talked; I sang again, then he talked; I sang again, then I talked.

Still the five hundred lamas sat immobile on their hassocks. We could not see their faces, but why did they not speak or make a move to end this meeting which looked as if it might go on all night?

I was on the verge of collapse, so I said in a low voice, "I will fall off this hassock in a minute."

"Then we will finish," Dr. Huang replied. And rising, we sailed out of the great hall.

Later we discovered that as guests we must be the first to move. Politeness demanded that our audience sat still as long as we sat!

Again I started to go to bed, but was disturbed by a knock on the door. Two priests stood outside.

"Woman, are you too tired to tell us more?" they asked humbly.

"Are you allowed to come into my room?"

"Yes, if there are two of us."

They came in, they listened intently and they went away.

A few minutes later two more came, and so it went on all night. Always the same question, "Will you explain how and why He died? Will you explain how it is He could love me?"

These men never questioned that God was the Creator of the world, they never doubted the fact of the virgin birth, they did not consider any of the miracles incredible. To them it was the wonder of God's love which obsessed them. The story of Christ's death on Calvary filled their minds with awe and reverence.

The next morning, when the priests were gathered in their temple, Dr. Huang and I had the opportunity of comparing notes, and I found that the same thing had happened in his room. Here, indeed, were men thirsting for the old, old story of God's wonderful plan of salvation.

We decided we would stay a little longer. We stayed a week; and all that time, whenever the men were free from their duties, they came and asked for more.

At last we decided we must leave the following day, so we announced that for the last night we would gladly talk to those who wanted to visit us. That evening I received a summons to go before the head lama whom we had not seen so far. Dr. Huang was not invited; I was to go alone.

The ordinary lamas were a kind of Chinese border race, but I imagined the head of such a large lamasery would surely be a true Tibetan, and I wondered how we would overcome the language difficulty.

I found a fine looking man, seated on a beautiful cushion, with servants attending him. To my amazement he addressed me in the pure Mandarin Chinese of Peking, which I understood perfectly.

We discussed various things, then greatly daring, I said, "Why did you let me—a foreign woman—come into your lamasery? Why did you allow me to speak to your priests?"

"It is a long story. Out on our mountainside grows a licorice herb which my lamas collect and sell in the cities. One year the men who had taken the herb harvest down on the mules were passing through a village when they saw a man waving a paper while he called out, 'Who wants one? Salvation free and for nothing. He who believes gets salvation and lives forever. If you want to learn more of this come to the gospel hall.'"

The lamas, utterly astounded at such a doctrine, took the tract and brought it back to the lamasery. I was then shown the tract, now worn and in pieces, stuck on the wall. It was a perfectly ordinary tract, simply quoting John 3:16, "For God so loved the world, that he gave his only begotten Son, that whosoever believeth in him should not perish, but have everlasting life."

That was all, but from it they had learned that somewhere there was a "God who loved." Everybody read it and reread it or had it read to them.

The head lama continued the story after I had read that important scrap of paper.

"The next year, when our men took the herb down to the cities they were told to find out where 'The God who loved' lived, but for five years they could learn nothing more.

"Then the man who had first received the tract vowed he would not come back until he learned more about this God. They went on and on until they came to Len Chow. There they saw an important-looking man on the street, and asked their usual question, 'Can you tell us where the God who loves lives?'

" 'Oh, yes,' he said. 'Go down that street, and you will come to a large gateway with three signs over it—"Faith, Hope, Charity." Go in there; they will tell you about God.'

"Jubilantly they approached the small China Inland Mission station and asked the same question of the Chinese evangelist. He told them all he could, then gave them each a copy of the Gospels.

"Eagerly they hurried back to the lamasery and we read the accounts of Matthew, Mark, Luke and John. We believed all that it contained, though there was much we could not understand. But one verse seemed of special importance. Christ had said, 'Go ye into all the world and preach the gospel,' so obviously one day someone would come to tell us more about this wonderful God. All we had to do was to wait and, when God sent a messenger, to be ready to receive him. For another three years we waited. Then two lamas, out on the hillside gathering sticks, heard someone singing. 'Those are the messengers we are waiting for,' they said. 'Only people who know God will sing.'

"While one went back to tell the rest of us to prepare for the long-expected guests, the other came down to meet you on the hillside."

That was why everything was done for our comfort, why they gladly clambered down and brought up our bundles, why they received us with hungry hearts.

We did not ask these men if they were saved; I do not know if they came out from the lamasery. I had preached His gospel in this place that God had appointed; I left the rest to Him and the work of the Holy Spirit.

No lamasery stands on that beautiful hillside now, for the Communists destroyed it and drove away all its inmates. What happened to those five hundred lamas, I often wonder. That many of them believed, trusted and received salvation, I have no shadow of doubt. God had prepared the soil; Dr. Huang and I were proud to be used as His messengers; only in eternity will we ever learn the result of one of the strangest weeks I have ever spent.

14

Mr. Shan

AFTER LEAVING THE LAMASERY there was no other course open to me but to turn back. Dr. Huang had said five days. We had already been away seventeen, and he had a wife and children at home. I could not go on alone in such a desolate, uninhabited country, so we returned to Tsin Tsui, witnessing to everyone we met on the road. From there I made my way back to Fenghsien to tell the students how wonderfully God had answered their prayers.

Some time later I was forced to go to a town of which I knew nothing at all. All I possessed was a ragged gown I had been given, and I felt utterly disappointed and puzzled. Why had God sent me to this strange city with no money? It was a huge city filled with students. What was there for me here?

I was taken in by a Chinese doctor and his wife and treated with great kindness. I was sitting in a room in their house when I became conscious that two men behind me were talk-

ing about some place in the city where there were people who
had never heard of Jesus Christ.

Completely forgetting my manners, I burst out, "Surely,
sirs, you must be mistaken. There are churches all over the
city; there are meetings everywhere; there are hundreds of
Christians."

"Madame, you must be a stranger to our city."

"I have been here only two days."

"We were talking of the prison."

"Is there a prison here?"

"Why, the second biggest prison in China is here, and no
one has ever been in there to tell the poor wretches of Jesus
Christ."

I talked further wth them but was not particularly disturbed. After all, prison work had nothing to do with me.
I had always preached in the villages and small towns—that
was my work.

But for the next few days I had no peace. God told me very
definitely that whether I liked it or not those men in the
prison were my business. Every one of them had a soul for
which Christ died, and I had come to China to proclaim that
gospel wherever God led me.

At the end of the week I sought an interview with the governor. He was exceedingly polite, but so patronizing that I
became increasingly nervous.

"What can I do for you, madame?" he asked, looking at
me coldly.

"Would you allow me to come into your prison and preach
about Jesus Christ to your prisoners?"

"You wish to come into the prison itself?"

"Yes."

"And what do you intend to do if I allow you to talk to the men?"

"I intend to alter your prison!"

"Madame, I have been governor for five years, and I have not altered it in the slightest degree."

"But I have Jesus Christ. It is He who can bring about the alteration."

I got my pass and I was escorted into the great prison courtyard. Rows and rows of horrible, dirty, cruel-faced, degraded men were lined up, with jailers at the end of each row. They were shouting, laughing and jeering.

I was so small that a kind of little mound had to be built up for me to stand on. I talked to them, I told them stories, then they trotted off. Day after day I stood on that little mound, my heart hammering wildly, but with the knowledge of the terrible, desperate need of these men driving me on.

Night after night I prayed for hours for them. Often when I should have been sleeping I was out on the hillside with a Christian leper, walking and praying, never daring to stop because he was "unclean" in body, but how truly clean in heart.

Besides going into the prison I was visiting the leper camp, and I believe it was the prayers of the Christian lepers which strengthened me during those first terrible weeks in the prison.

At last one prisoner was converted, then another, until I had five who would come and take their place beside me and testify to the change God had brought about in their lives.

This was wonderful, but the prison certainly wasn't altered, and there were thousands still mocking at God's Word.

One day I had finished talking and was going out feeling hurt, tired and longing to get away from the awful stench of unclean humanity, when the gate opened and four men were dragged in. They were chained together, and were thrown violently on the ground by their guards, who stood over them with guns.

My first thought was *Get out of this as fast as you can.*

I hurried toward the gate when a voice said, "Gladys Aylward, I died for these just as I did for you."

I turned back to the guard. "Will you allow me to speak to these men?"

Roughly, and in impolite language, the guard refused. I walked slowly around the courtyard, praying, then I asked again.

This time I received a curse for my answer, and the guard shouted, "Throw this pestering woman out." I was put firmly out by the gateman.

A few days later I learned that all four men were murderers. Three were already dead; only one, Mr. Shan, was still alive. Mr. Shan was young, handsome and arrogant, but there was something about him I felt to be utterly evil. He looked at me in a horribly offensive fashion and said unrepeatable things. I disliked him intensely, but I prayed for him and I got my friends to pray for him. One day I tried to speak to him, but with an oath he turned and spat in my face, and I felt I almost hated him.

The months went by, and now I had others helping me in the work. Other prisoners were converted and we had forty in a class preparing for baptism. But still the blessing had not swept through the prison and changed it to any noticeable degree, but in the leper colony prayer went on incessantly.

One day after I had finished speaking, the men formed into their lines to return to their cells. They always had to move at a trot, and not one could speak while moving.

I stood watching them pass, my heart aching for them. By now I knew most of these men. I knew why they were in this place and, though not allowed to speak, I could smile and nod.

Way down the line I saw the man I disliked so much—Mr. Shan, the man who seemed harder to move than the prison walls themselves.

Very clearly a voice said, "Speak to that man!"

"Oh, no," I replied. "He despises me! He actually spat at me. Besides, the law of the prison states I must not speak to him while the line is moving."

"Nevertheless, you must speak to him."

What was I to do? A cold sweat broke over me. He was almost up to me. I was so agitated that I leaned forward and let my hand fall on his shoulder, while I burst out, "Oh, Mr. Shan, aren't you miserable?"

Of all the stupid remarks, I thought immediately.

With a horrible curse he threw off my hand. "What is it to do with you if I am miserable?"

"Because I am so happy."

"Of course you are. Doesn't the door open for you whenever you want to go out?"

"Ah, that isn't the reason. It is because Jesus Christ died for me."

Mr. Shan passed on, and I realized the awful thing I had done. One of China's greatest unwritten laws is that no woman touches a man in public.

I left that prison depressed and ashamed. Before those men I had defiled myself and with such a man as Mr. Shan!

Mr. Shan followed the line and sat on a stone in an inner courtyard, his head bowed in his hands. A few moments later, Dhu Cor, the first man who had been converted in the prison, saw him sitting there.

"Are you going to be ill?" he asked, staring at him closely.

"Did you see what *she* did?"

"What?"

"She touched me."

"No. That is a lie!"

"It is no lie. She put her hand on my shoulder."

"I cannot believe it."

Another prisoner who had been listening joined in. "What he says is true. She *did* touch him."

"She touched me as if she loved me!" Mr. Shan gasped.

"Perhaps she does love you," Dhu Cor replied.

"What, a clean woman like her love me, a murderer, who has cursed her and spat at her!"

"Yes, I believe she could because she believes that God loves you no matter what you have done."

* * *

Mr. Shan was converted, not because of a great sermon, but because years ago in London God had taken a girl and asked her to give Him her hands, her feet, her whole body for

His use, and that day God had touched Mr. Shan through that poor human instrument.

Mr. Shan's conversion began the real revival in that prison. Men spent hours listening to the Word of God; they spent hours on their knees; and we had baptisms which lasted three days.

Testimonies, especially that of Mr. Shan, were printed in the prison press, and before long calls came in from other prisons to come and do the same as had been done here.

The governor himself, convinced by the alteration in even the most hardened criminals, was converted, and proclaimed in no uncertain fashion that what he had been unable to do in five years, the power of the glorious gospel of salvation had accomplished in one.

15

Even unto Death

WHILE THE WORK at the leper colony and the prison was going on I heard that the Methodist church was advertising for an evangelist who could deal with the great crowds of refugees who were pouring into the city, most of whom came, like myself, from the north.

I applied for this job, but stipulated that I should be allowed to carry on my work in the prison and leper camp. This was agreed, and I went to live in a room at the back of the church.

During all these months one or two of my children were usually with me, but only the older ones who could look after themselves. I was glad of their companionship, and it was good to feel that I had some sort of family life.

The war had just ended, and most of the missionaries had gone home or were still in concentration camps. The need was so great, but the workers so few!

There seemed to be a spiritual lethargy about this church

to which I was now attached which weighed on me heavily. The building itself was neglected and in a filthy condition. It was a large church, with a huge gallery, and one day I determined to go up there to see what it contained.

I found that, like the temple in Nehemiah's day, it had been used as a storeroom. It was full of old junk, and everywhere there was rubbish, dirt and cobwebs.

As I stood looking over the balcony, feeling discouraged and depressed, the sun suddenly came in at the dusty window. A shaft of golden light struck the cross on the communion table, and as I looked I saw the Lord stand there looking up at me.

As I gazed, He spoke. "Prepare this place for Me, for I intend to bless."

Leaning further forward, I said, "O Lord, how long?"

"Forty days" came back the reply, and gradually the vision faded.

I knelt down, my heart throbbing with reverence and awe. I truly believed that in forty days blessing would come, but before that I had to work and pray. I resolved that every day I would wash and clean as much of the church as I could, and when I had cleaned it I would pray in that part.

For some time I had not been well, and some Christian friends had arranged that I should go away with them for a rest and vacation. I began my cleaning and praying, but I told no one of my vision and my resolve.

As the time drew near for my proposed vacation, I grew perturbed. Only a few of the forty days had passed; how could I disobey my Lord's commands? I decided to tell our

Chinese pastor, Christian Shang, about it. He did not ridicule my story but immediately agreed to join me in the task.

I went to see the friends with whom I was to go on vacation, and found that they had completely forgotten the arrangement and their promise. They felt most embarrassed and were deeply apologetic. I almost shouted "Hallelujah!" The Lord had overruled even in this small detail. I could stay on until the blessing came.

As Christian Shang and I were working in the church one day, Gordon, one of my adopted sons, came to look for me. He, too, joined in the scrubbing and praying. A few days later the treasurer of the church, Chen Tsung, found us; and last, a converted bandit joined our "work party." So now five of us spent every available minute washing, cleaning and praying. By the end of the forty days the church was spotless and we had prayed in every part of it. But we knew that if we were to have blessing we must work outside too, so we decided we would have special gospel campaigns, and during the following months we were wonderfully blessed.

About this time we had a request from the Youth for Christ organization to hold a campaign. They would pay all expenses if we could supply the workers.

By now we had a band of keen converts who gladly did whatever was necessary, and we had a church fit to be used. Bob Pearce, an American, was the evangelist, and Dr. Andrew Gih, the interpreter. And because the ground had been prepared by incessant, earnest prayer, the blessing swept through the city. Hundreds were truly converted, including many university students.

For several months we continued in glorious blessing. It

almost seemed that we had gone back to the days of the early church, but we know now that God was strengthening us and preparing us for the terrible days that were to lie ahead for all of us, young and old alike.

The Communist party took complete control of the university, and to each of the five hundred students was handed a long form on which was a series of questions to be answered truthfully. I managed to get hold of one of these forms and, because I wanted to understand just what they involved, I tried to fill it in. Some of the questions were awkward, some seemingly irrelevant and utterly ridiculous, such as "Do you know what your grandmother died of? How many children did your uncle have? How much money did your grandfather have when he died?"

There was no mention of religion, no mention of a political party; but right at the end, when one was tired and confused, came the all-important question.

"What position are you in? If for the government, put a circle, if against, put an ✕."

This was the question which meant either compliance with all the authorities decreed, or future unpleasantness. If one put an ✕ it would mean he would be outside the party, he would have no job, he would be poor, he would be an outcast.

Almost all of those five hundred students had started their education in Christian schools. If they had been ill, they had gone to Christian hospitals, because all that was good in health and education had come to the isolated districts of China through the missions. Also, many had been converted during the recent campaigns.

When the five hundred forms were counted, three hundred had put circles, two hundred had put an ✕! The Communists looked grave. They called together the three hundred who had signed agreement with those in power, and told them that there was work for them to do. They could use what methods they liked—except that of actually taking life—to force those two hundred into line.

For the next month the most horrible forms of teasing, petty cruelty and unpleasant irritations went on. Then the forms were handed out again. But to the utter amazement of the authorities, there were fewer circles and more ✕'s!

How had this happened? They began to make urgent inquiries and they learned that every morning the Christian students had held prayer meetings.

In the university the lectures began at nine o'clock. All the students lived in the campus, and at eight they went to breakfast, but at seven the Christians had gathered in groups for prayer and Bible reading in order to gain strength for the day of testing they knew lay before them.

When the non-Christians had discovered this, they had broken up the group and caused pandemonium. So the Christians gathered at six o'clock. Again their opponents discovered them, so they rose even earlier and met at five o'clock.

So it went on, until by the end of the month some of the Christians were getting hardly any sleep.

The authorities took immediate action. "We'll stop all this congregating together. We'll put an end to all this prayer and Bible reading," they announced.

Each Christian was isolated and put under the guard of ten red-hot Communists for three months. Their every movement was watched, and night and day they were talked at, jeered at, indoctrinated.

We watched these poor isolated Christians getting paler, thinner and more haggard. There was no way of contacting them, and we trembled for them. They were young in years and many of them only babes in the Christian faith, but all we could do was pray for them that their faith would not fail in spite of all the fiery darts of the wicked one.

At the end of the three months we were all forced to appear in the market square. Under a huge squad of Communist police we saw the two hundred students marched into the square. In a witness box stood a man with a list of names. He called out the first.

A girl of seventeen stepped forward. She was refined and beautiful, and had been brought up in one of those lovely courtyards that belonged to the wealthy of Peking before the war. She had been sent here for safety—now she stood before her accusers!

"What position are you standing in now?" bellowed the voice of the man in the box.

She walked to the little platform. She faltered a little and we thought she was going to fall. Why put this slim, frail slip of a girl up first? we questioned. Poor child, how can she stand?

Then her voice rang out, suddenly clear and strong. "Sir, when I went for my three months' indoctrination I thought Jesus Christ was real. I thought the Bible was true. Now I *know* Jesus Christ is real, I *know* this Book is true!"

One after the other of those two hundred names were called out, and not one faltered, though they knew enough of their persecutors by now to know that they would be made to suffer.

Every one of them was beheaded that very day in the marketplace. Before each execution the victim was given one last chance to recant; but even those at the end, who had been forced to watch the terrible butchery of all the others, did not flinch.

"Why," people ask, "did God allow it?" Was it because He loved them so much that He took them before worse terrors and tortures befell them? Theirs, maybe, was the easier death. They went straight to those many mansions their Saviour had gone before to prepare for them. They had followed Him even unto death.

16

Back to England

FOR A LONG TIME I had been oppressed with the feeling that I ought to return to England. It had been twenty years since I left, and long ago I had decided that it was unlikely I would ever return. I was Chinese now in name, in dress, even—in some ways—in thought, and I loved my adopted race. I was needed here, and it had never occurred to me that England needed evangelists maybe even more than China.

After the great blessing in the Methodist Church and in the prison, the newly converted held many prayer meetings. They felt led to pray for definite things. And if one Christian had a specific need on his heart, he voiced it and they prayed on and on about it.

One day I was attending one of these prayer meetings when a young man stated that he felt very definite and earnest prayer was needed for England. At the end I took this young man aside and asked why he had brought the subject before the Christians.

135

"Don't you think England needs praying for?" he asked.

"Yes, but not as if it is a heathen land, because, after all, it is a Christian country."

"But are they having blessing and revival?"

"I do not know."

"They can't be. If they were we would know it—in the midst of all our famine, war and suffering. England, the land that sent us the gospel, is worshiping other gods."

"What do you mean?"

"To them sport, film stars, wealth, amusement—all are far more important than God."

"But how do you know all this?"

"From the papers. I will bring you some to prove it."

A little later he handed me a bundle of Chinese papers, and when I read them I understood the burden of his prayers. Every item of reported news from England, every picture, was concerned with a film star, or a sportsman, or a horse race—not one mention of God. England, seemingly so prosperous while other countries passed through terrible suffering at the hands of Communist domination, had forgotten what was all-important—the realization that God mattered in the life of a nation no less than in that of an individual.

From that time I knew that I must go back to the land of my birth. I must return to do what I could to dispel the spiritual lethargy that had overtaken so many. I must testify to the great faith of the Chinese church. I must let people know what great things God had done for me.

Some months later I applied for a permit, but the quota was full so I had to wait a whole year before I could apply again. By that time things were getting very hot. I knew I was under suspicion, and I set off for Shanghai. I had no money and no clothes, but I knew of a society that might help me.

This society was composed of a few godly Chinese who had banded together to help the destitute German missionaries. During the Second World War these Germans had suffered terribly. They could receive no help from Germany and, of course, got no help from the English because they were enemies. At the end of war this society paid the passage home to Germany for those who were able to go, but many had died of starvation and disease.

To these Chinese Christians I owe the fact that I ever set foot in England again. I had gone to China with very little except youthful determination. I came back, middle-aged, with absolutely nothing but the knowledge that God had never failed me. Maybe I would find many things strange and difficult; but if God had work for me here, He would supply all that was necessary and lead me a step at a time.

17

Wong Kwai

WHEN I RETURNED TO BRITAIN after an absence of over twenty years I felt almost as foreign as I had felt when I first went to China.

I had taken Chinese nationality years ago, I wore Chinese dress, I ate Chinese food. I even thought as Chinese people think. I came back to a Britain very different from the one I had left—a war-scarred country, with a carelessness concerning morals that shocked me.

Here in this land with churches or chapels in almost every street, with thousands of ministers, there was a terrible apathy. I had watched hundreds of Chinese Christians, who only a few years ago had been idol worshipers, suffer terrible privations, even torture and death for their faith. How would our so-called Christian land react if the Communist scourge attacked it?

Even in the churches themselves, the Christians appeared lukewarm. The women were dressed in the height of fashion, and social events were of much greater importance than the prayer meeting or the spread of the gospel message. It was far harder to reach the hearts of an English congregation than those of the ignorant, heathen Chinese.

I could not go back to China because of Communist persecution, but how often I longed for the uncomplicated life we had lived in Yangcheng before war and the powers of evil had swept across my adopted country.

But I felt God had brought me back for a purpose, and before long He opened up many avenues of service. I had requests from Christian groups all over the country to tell my story. This entailed traveling hundreds of miles which I did not mind, and writing scores of letters which I hated.

I found, too, that there were many Chinese people in England, and I realized how lonely they must feel in this strange country. I spoke their language and wore their dress and, like them, had to report to the police as an alien. I began to seek them out. There were scores in London and, in time, we formed a small Chinese Christian church. We had a Chinese worker who met the ships as they came from Hong Kong and Singapore, and we did our best to make the Chinese sailors welcome. Through them I got news of my beloved, unhappy China, and sometimes had messages smuggled through from some of my children. And, oh, the joy of knowing that even under Communist domination the seeds that had been sown in their hearts had been uncrushed. Jesus Christ was still their all in all.

In Bristol and Liverpool I found Chinese in great numbers, and I had the joy of leading some of them to Christ and witnessing their baptism.

I had been asked to visit Ireland several times, but I had not felt led to accept the invitation. Yet one more request came in and I felt that for some reason the Lord wanted me to visit Belfast.

When the boat drew in, I noticed a police inspector and two constables come aboard. A few minutes later a steward approached me and asked me to go to the captain's cabin. There I found the police contingent.

"Madame, the inspector has been informed that a foreign alien is on this ship, but the only person answering to that description is yourself," the captain said half apologetically.

I laughed, then explained that I was English but had been in China as a missionary for over twenty years. Now, driven out by the Communists, I was back in my native land. But, as I had taken on Chinese nationality, I was regarded as an alien.

"Rather an awkward situation," the inspector said, stroking his chin. "What have I to put on the form? A little English lady, dressed in Chinese clothes, coming to speak in a church —nothing we can hold you for in that, is there?"

I laughed again. "I've been in prison in Russia and in China, so I guess an Irish one won't be so bad."

The men grinned in friendly fashion, then the inspector said jovially, "Well, as I can't take you to prison, how about allowing us to drive you to where you are staying?"

"I'll be very grateful," I replied with an inward sigh of relief that things had gone so easily.

I drove in state to my host's house. As I shook hands with the inspector, he said, "Now, if there is anything at all I can do for you while you are in our city, don't hesitate to let me know."

I thanked him, but felt that there was little likelihood of my needing police protection here.

The next day as I walked down the street I met a Chinese girl. We greeted each other like sisters, and I talked to her for a long time and invited her to the meetings I was having.

"Are there any other Chinese in this town?" I asked as we were about to part.

"Yes, three others," she replied.

"Can you give me their addresses so that I can visit them?" I asked.

She wrote down the information, then added, "There is one more Chinese woman here, but you won't be interested in her as she is in the mental asylum."

We said farewell and I went on my way. At the first opportunity I would visit these other people but, of course, the one in the asylum did not concern me.

I went to my room and knelt to pray, but something seemed to hinder me. Then quite clearly a voice said to me, "That woman you heard about *is* your concern. That is why I brought you to Ireland."

I went downstairs and asked my host how I could get in touch with a patient in an asylum. He replied that he had a friend who had access to the place as he was on its board of managers.

The friend kindly offered to drive me to the asylum the next day, and to inform the matron as to why we were coming. Just before I had left home I had received a parcel, and in it had been a Chinese moon cake. I put it into my bag when we left to visit the asylum.

I was introduced to the matron, who handed me over to a nurse. She took me into a room and said she would bring the woman I wished to see. Then she said a strange thing.

"Miss Aylward, I believe 'this woman is as sane as you or I. You will be doing God's work if you can help her."

At that moment a nurse half dragged in one of the saddest specimens of Chinese womanhood I had ever seen—thin, frightened, cringing like a whipped dog.

I spoke to her in Chinese, but she did not raise her eyes. I tried to tell her I wanted to help her, but still there was no response.

Then, on impulse, I took the moon cake from my bag and slipped it into her hand. She stared at it, and a queer, strangled gasp came from her lips.

"A moon cake," she said in Chinese. Then she looked at me and I smiled.

"Wong Kwai, I want to help you," I said. "I too am Chinese now. Can you tell me how you got here? Tell me how I can help you."

She stared at me a long time; then from her pocket she pulled a bundle of letters.

"Can you read?" she whispered.

I nodded.

"From my son, but I cannot read them," she said in a tragic little voice.

I opened one and read it—a simple little letter from a dutiful son begging his mother to tell him where she was and why he had heard nothing from her.

Long before I had finished, Wong Kwai was trembling, then sobbing in a quiet, hopeless sort of way.

I let her cry for a while, then I said gently, "Now tell me how you got here and I will write to your son for you."

So by degrees the story came out. She had been engaged in China by an Irish captain and his wife to act as nurse to their two small children, and had come home with them. Then they had left her with the children in the home of the captain's mother while they went visiting in England. The old grandmother was a bigoted Irish woman who hated all foreigners, looking on them as spies and fifth columnists. She could not speak Chinese, and Wong Kwai could not speak English, so before long trouble started. Wong Kwai said the grandmother used to fly into terrible rages, and one day set on Wong Kwai, who tried to defend herself. The grandmother immediately sent for the police and declared that this Chinese devil was a raving lunatic and had attacked her. She dare not keep her in the house a moment longer.

Poor Wong Kwai could not understand what was being said, but the sight of the police terrified her. When they took hold of her to take her away, she screamed and kicked in frenzied terror. There was no one to speak for her, no one could understand her, so she was put into the asylum, and proved tremendously useful as "a sweeping woman." For months she had stayed there, a lonely, sad, bewildered little creature.

Then I began the struggle to get her released, and suddenly I remembered the promise of my police inspector. He could surely help in this matter. And he was as good as his word.

He even found out that her employer was chargeable for her return fare to Hong Kong, as only on that undertaking was he allowed to bring her from China.

I had to make myself personally responsible for Mrs. Wong's conduct and sign numerous papers, but at last she was free, and I could take her home to England to my flat where my friend Rosemary and I could treat her once more as a human being. And how she blossomed under our care and love!

We never preached at her, but she listened to our prayers and loved to hear me read the Bible stories in Chinese. Then one day she came with her face glowing. "Ai-weh-deh, there is peace in here, because now Jesus is here," she said, pressing her hand to her breast.

My own heart sang for her as I looked at her. What a change from the miserable little stray I had first seen.

A few days later Mrs. Wong returned with another Chinese woman, Mrs. Cheng, whom she had met on the street. "I must tell her about my Jesus," she said. And as she puttered about in the kitchen I could hear her explaining in her own simple fashion about the wonderful things that Jesus had done for her.

A few days before Christmas Mrs. Cheng accepted the Saviour, and together those two little women set out to work for their Lord wherever they could meet a fellow countryman.

* * *

At that time I was feeling very tired after a long series of meetings. Mrs. Rosemary Brisco, who had provided a home for me and had worked very hard also for the cause of China, agreed wholeheartedly when I suggested that we should have a quiet Christmas for once, just Rosemary, myself and Wong Kwai.

Wong Kwai laughed when I repeated my suggestion in Chinese. She had come to know our house by now and knew it was seldom quiet.

The next day Rosemary said, "I have been thinking about poor Mrs. Cheng. She's all alone, we could ask her for Christmas day, couldn't we? Our little chicken will stretch to four."

That evening Peter, a Chinese boy who was very shy, came to see me. "What are you doing for Christmas, Peter?" I asked.

"Well, nothing," he replied.

I looked at Rosemary and I could read the words "My poor little chicken!" in her eyes, but she nodded.

"Then spend Christmas with us, Peter," and his shy brown eyes lit up.

Before he left, Alan, a French boy who had recently been converted, arrived, and somehow before he left Alan had also been added to our guests.

Early the next morning there was a telegram from Jane, the Chinese girl in Ireland who had first told me about Wong Kwai being in the mental home. Jane asked if she could come for Christmas and duly arrived the next day.

"My poor little chicken!" Rosemary sighed. "It is getting smaller and smaller!"

Wong Kwai, however, laughed gaily, thrilled at the thought of her first Christmas as a Christian spent among so many of her own country folk.

On Christmas Eve the bell rang and Wong Kwai, who loved answering the door, rushed to open it. We heard her voice rise in joyful surprise, and I translated for Rosemary.

"She says the boys have come," I whispered. "What boys is she talking about?"

Wong Kwai rushed into the room, her face beaming, and behind her stood three smiling Chinese youths.

"The boys have come," chanted Wong Kwai. "The boys have come from Hong Kong."

"The boys" came forward and bowed low to each of us in turn. Then one who seemed to be the leader explained, "There are sixteen in our party. We are all students, boys and girls, from Hong Kong. Just before the ship landed one of the passengers explained that tomorrow is Christmas. All the shops will be closed and the colleges will not be open, so we did not know what to do. Then one boy remembered that before we left home, a young man had said to him that if he was in difficulty in England go to one of these addresses."

He handed me a piece of paper and I saw that one address was in Leeds, one in Manchester, the other was my own.

"We three came to find you; the rest stayed with the luggage," the leader explained.

"We must see what we can do," I said, and Rosemary and I began to plan ways and means. It was impossible for us to provide beds, but not far away there was a hostel that might take them in. I went over and found the landlady willing to have them to sleep, but she could not provide food at such short notice.

So our family had swollen with a vengeance, and even the next morning some others were added. Rosemary's poor little chicken was smothered in great bowls of rice, and Wong

Kwai, in her element, spent the day cooking pot after pot of Chinese food.

Our quiet Christmas was only a dream. I can't even remember tasting a piece of chicken, for our guests finally numbered twenty-seven. But what did food matter compared with the great happiness that packed our little home that day, and the blessing of God that followed.

Soon after this Mrs. Wong decided that there was work for her at home.

"My son does not know about Jesus," she said. "My aunt who lives up on the hill has not heard of Him; I must go back and tell them, and many others too."

So Mrs. Wong left us, and how much we missed her happy helpful presence.

Weeks later we received a letter from her son together with a beautiful gown for myself. He was full of thanks for all we had done for his mother, and said she wished him to say that she still had peace and was telling everyone about her wonderful Jesus.

18

An Old Suit

AFTER I HAD BEEN BACK in England a short while I began to remember all the Chinese who had practically nothing to wear. Hundreds had been driven from their homes and had crowded into Free China. Many had left the mainland and gone to Formosa or other islands. They were herded together in far worse conditions than our farm animals. Even in organized refugee camps the food was meager, and there were few extra clothes to be doled out when the rags that had been worn for months dropped off.

I looked at the English people, wrapped up in their warm winter clothes in spite of clothing coupons and utility material. I saw no one in desperate need of either food or clothing. In fact, there was far less hardship than there had been when I left England years ago, for at that time we had great lines of unemployed, and many men, women and children were undernourished and ill-clad.

As I traveled around speaking in various churches, I told

of the desperate plight of many of the Chinese Christians. And before long, parcels of outgrown or discarded clothing came pouring in.

I was sharing a home in London with my dear friend, Mrs. Rosemary Brisco. Once our small house had been part of the mews* belonging to the large homes of society grandees who had their London houses in Bryanston Square. Now the mews were no longer needed, so the stables were turned into very cozy little apartments, each with its own small garage.

We had no car so the garage was the storeroom for the secondhand garments we received.

Rosemary was a lady by birth and had a very different education and background from my own, but she made no fuss about sorting out the conglomeration of stuff which we collected each week. She could not preach and had never been to China, but she loved the Chinese who visited us and was just as interested as I in every aspect of the work.

While I was attending meetings up and down the country, Rosemary would be busy sorting out, washing, mending and packing such things as were suitable to send abroad. It wasn't a spectacular job, but we will never know how much comfort it brought to those poor homeless people.

Just before the big Christmas postal rush, we sent off fifteen parcels weighing twenty-five pounds each to a Norwegian lady missionary who was working in a huge refugee camp just outside the Communist territory.

As always, when the consignment of parcels arrived and before they were opened, the missionary arranged a special

*Stables, carriage garages and living quarters built around a court or street or yard.

prayer meeting so that they might pray for guidance in the distribution of these clothes.

That evening the missionary met a Christian Chinese merchant who told her he traveled between Hong Kong and Macao with his goods.

"Are there many refugees in Macao?" she inquired.

"The place is absolutely packed with them," was the reply.

"Is there any Christian work being done among them?"

"No one is allowed to do anything because Macao belongs to the Portuguese."

"Will you take one of these parcels and pray that you will be guided to give the clothes to those most in need?"

So, with one of the unopened bundles, the merchant set off for Macao. He had a room in the town, and he went straight to it to leave his belongings. Then he decided to go out to buy some food. Coming down the street he met a man who looked ill and starved, yet carried himself proudly in spite of the fact that all he wore on his emaciated body were a sleeveless waistcoat and a pair of ladies' panties!

The merchant stared, then gasped. This man had once been one of China's most prominent men.

"Sir, are you looking for lodgings?" the merchant asked diffidently.

The stranger shook his head.

"Would you come and eat with me?" went on the merchant.

"Thank you, I accept," was the dignified reply.

Together they went to a small eating house and the merchant ordered a simple meal.

"I recognized you as you came down the street," the merchant remarked as the meal progressed. "Is there anything I can do to help you?"

"I believe you are a Christian. Will you pray with me?"

The merchant bowed his head, and very simply the nobleman said, "O Lord, thank You for answering the first two parts of my prayer. You have brought me to safety; You have given me something to eat. Now please answer the third part and give me something to wear so that I can get employment and so keep my self-respect."

"I believe God has answered that prayer already," the merchant said eagerly. "Come home with me now."

Together they opened the bundle which we had sent from London with our loving prayers, and there, right on top, lay something which had very seldom come into our hands—a man's complete suit! Often we had odd jackets or odd trousers, but practically never a matching suit.

Weeks later we received a letter from Macao, bearing the signature of a man who had been one of China's wealthiest and most influential men before the Communists came into power and robbed him of home, money and family.

In that letter were many grateful thanks for the clothes he had received, and through which he had been able to gain employment. Now he was hoping to save a little money so he could help his wife and family to escape and join him once more.

He told how he, a prominent Buddhist, had been stripped of all he possessed, then thrown into prison. But it was there he had come to know Jesus Christ as his Saviour and Lord.

He had lost all in this world, but he had peace and joy in his heart because he was a Christian, and nothing the enemy could do could take that from him.

It was letters such as this one, and the deep longing in my heart to see some of my children again, which made me determined to leave the comfortable, safe shores of England and go once more to share the hazards of the people I loved so much.

I could not return to Communist China, but I could go to Formosa and Hong Kong, and many of my loved ones had escaped to these places.

I felt I had finished my work in Britain. I had traveled far and wide telling of the sufferings of the Chinese Christians, and now I wanted to tell the gospel story once more in places where it was no easy thing to be a Christian. I was getting older and felt that the years I had left had to be given to my Chinese people.

When I arrived I was given a wonderful welcome—how different from that first time I landed on Mrs. Lawson's doorstep in Yangcheng. What a joy it was to be met by many of my children, now grownup and with families of their own, but still true to their Saviour. And what a tremendous thrill it was to be summoned to an audience with Madame Chiang Kai-shek herself, and to be thanked by her publicly for what I had done for the children of China.

The conditions under which many of the Nationalist Chinese were living horrified me, and the sufferings which many of the refugees had undergone almost broke my heart. There was so much work to do, and I had so little with which to do it. With a handful of other Christians I began a mission in the refugee area of Hong Kong, and an orphanage near Taipeh, but there was no money for even the necessities.

Then came frequent calls from America to go and tell Christians there of the work, and eventually I felt that this was what God would have me do. Of my own choice I would have preferred to stay with my loved ones and share their privations, but it seemed that by going to America I could help in a more practical way. Churches in many parts offered me the use of their pulpits, and promised support. So once more I set out for a strange country, knowing little of its customs or its people, but from the first they took me to their hearts and never have I spoken to more appreciative audiences.

And again God has proved that if we trust Him He will provide, for the organization known as World Vision Incorporated has undertaken by faith to supply money for the support of the mission in Hong Kong and the orphanage near Taipeh.

My heart is full of praise that one so insignificant, uneducated and ordinary in every way could be used to His glory and for the blessing of His people in poor persecuted China.